AF686354

university of
groningen

Measuring The Costs Of Chapter 11 Cases

Professional Fees in American Corporate Bankruptcy Cases

Proefschrift

ter verkrijging van het doctoraat in de
Rechtsgeleerdheid
aan de Rijksuniversiteit Groningen
op gezag van de
Rector Magnificus, dr. F. Zwarts,
in het openbaar te verdedigen op
donderdag 25 november 2010
om 16.15 uur

door
Stephen James Lubben
geboren op 30 augustus 1971
te Massachusetts, Verenigde Staten van Amerika

Promotor:	Prof. dr. O. Couwenberg
Beoordelingscommissie:	Prof. dr. A. de Jong Prof. mr. B. Lawless Prof. mr. F.M. J. Verstijlen

Measuring The Costs Of Chapter 11 Cases

Professional Fees in American Corporate Bankruptcy Cases

Stephen J. Lubben
Daniel J. Moore Professor of Law
Seton Hall University School of Law

Eleven International Publishing
The Hague
2010

Published, sold and distributed by Eleven International Publishing
P.O. Box 85576
2508 CG The Hague
The Netherlands
Tel.: +31 70 33 070 33
Fax: +31 70 33 070 30
Website: www.elevenpub.com

Eleven International Publishing is an imprint of Boom uitgevers Den Haag.

Cover design: Primo!Studio, Delft
Layout: Textcetera, Den Haag

© 2010 S.J. Lubben | Eleven International Publishing, The Hague

This publication is protected by international copyright law.
All rights reserved. No part of this publication may be reproduced, stored in a retrieval system, or transmitted in any form or by any means, electronic, mechanical, photocopying, recording or otherwise, without the prior permission of the publisher.

ISBN 978-90-8974-370-1
NUR 828

Acknowledgements

This dissertation is probably unlike most others, in that the author is already a tenured professor. Thus, much of the anxiety normally associated with the project was absent, and instead I found the project to be a joy.

My advisor and promoter, Prof. Dr. Oscar Couwenberg, deserves much of the credit for making the project so enjoyable. Not only did he guide me through the unfamiliar waters of the Dutch university system, but his comments on each of the chapters greatly improved the end result. Hopefully much future collaboration is yet to come.

Many thanks also to the members of my dissertation committee, Abe de Jong, Robert Lawless and Frank M.J. Verstijlen, Seton Hall University School of Law and Dean Patrick Hobbs, for supporting my sabbatical project, the New York Society Library, where I wrote much of this dissertation, Bloomberg LP, which provided some additional data for this project, and Ana Santos and Silvia Cardoso at Seton Hall for their help in formatting this manuscript.

I should also thank Professor Elizabeth Warren, my LL.M. thesis advisor ten years ago at Harvard Law School, who first got me interested in measuring the costs of chapter 11, and the late Professor Clark Byse, of both Harvard and Boston University School of Law, who first got me interested in becoming a law professor.

I am extremely appreciative of the support of my family. My daughter Vivian simply wants it to be known that she helped. Our dog Myrna, whom I still miss very much, faithfully slept by my side while Oscar and I planned the early stages of this project.

As always, my greatest thanks go to my wife, Jennifer Hoyden, who has edited, corrected, and improved this manuscript from start to finish. She plays the biggest part in everything I do.

Stephen J. Lubben
Friday, June 4, 2010

* * *

This dissertation is based in part on data gathered by the author as part of the ABI Chapter 11 Professional Fee Study, which was funded by a grant from the American Bankruptcy Institute, the ABI Endowment Fund, and the National Conference of Bankruptcy Judges. I am grateful for the ABI and NCBJ's assistance with this project. All conclusions are my own and do not necessarily reflect the views of the ABI or the NCBJ or their members.

Contents

1 Introduction

The costs of corporate reorganization are strangely compelling in a financial crisis, or even a run of the mill recession. The hundreds of millions of dollars paid by "bankrupt" or "insolvent" firms like Lehman Brothers, or Enron before it, merely to address their situation often seems quite odd to the casual reader of the *Wall Street Journal*, who still thinks of bankruptcy as the equivalent of corporate death.[1]

A similar phenomenon can be seen in the academic literature, dating back to at least Modigliani and Miller in 1958, and the notion that a firm's capital structure amounts to little more than slices in a pie.[2] In this world, debtor-firms are typically discussed relative to a backdrop of complete contracts and zero transactions cost s.[3] Accordingly, firms that encounter financial distress – that is, having liquid assets insufficient to meet current fixed claims – simply renegotiate their obligations and proceed accordingly.[4] Slight deviations from the background assumptions can be assumed and then addressed by neatly automated responses.[5] That Kmart, a large discount store chain, would pay more than $134 million to professionals to do so is inconsistent with this idealized understanding of the world, and thus each dollar spent is deemed evidence of inefficiency.

Of course, both views of "bankruptcy" are based on basic misunderstanding or gross oversimplification. Both assume that financial distress is costless, whereas even liquidation does not happen by itself.[6] Indeed, only abandonment of a distressed firm might be costless – if we limit our conception of cost to actual "out of pocket" expenditures by the debtor-firm.[7]

1 Throughout I follow American practice and use "bankruptcy" to refer to the insolvency or failure of a business entity – typically a corporation – cognizant of the fact that in some jurisdictions bankruptcy only refers to the financial distress of individuals.

2 Franco Modigliani & Merton H. Miller, *The Cost of Capital, Corporation Finance, and the Theory of Investment*, 48 Am. Econ. Rev. 261, 297 (1958). See generally John D. Ayer, *The Role of Finance Theory in Shaping Bankruptcy Policy*, 3 Am. Bankr. Inst. L. Rev. 53 (1995) ("Modigliani and Miller argue . . . that under defined assumptions it makes no difference what the debt-equity structure might be-the value of the firm remains the same in any event.").

3 *See* Robert A. Haugen & Lemma W. Senbet, *The Insignificance of Bankruptcy Costs to the Theory of Optimal Capital Structure*, 33 J. Fin. 383, 386 (1978). See also Jonathan B. Berk et al., *Human Capital, Bankruptcy, and Capital Structure*, 65 J. Fin. 891 (2010).

4 See, e.g., Barry E. Adler, *Finance's Theoretical Divide and the Proper Role of Insolvency Rules*, 67 S. Cal. L. Rev. 1107, 1131 (1994).

5 *E.g.*, Barry E. Adler & Ian Ayres, *A Dilution Mechanism for Valuing Corporations in Bankruptcy*, 111 Yale L.J. 83 (2001); Lucian Arye Bebchuk, *A New Approach to Corporate Reorganizations*, 101 Harv. L. Rev. 775 (1988).

6 *See* Donald R. Korobkin, *The Unwarranted Case Against Corporate Reorganization: A Reply to Bradley and Rosenzweig*, 78 Iowa L. Rev. 669, 720 (1993).

7 *Cf.* Kathryn R. Heidt, *The Automatic Stay in Environmental Bankruptcies*, 67 Am. Bankr. L.J. 69, 121 (1993).

More broadly, understanding the cost of a corporate reorganization system is important because debtor-firms face the reality of a world with incomplete contracts, incomplete information, uncertain asset values, and complex capital structures that highlight the many ways in which assumptions about capital structure irrelevance or managerial rationality, or both, fail.[8] Given these truths, and the added reality of asset market disruptions,[9] it is generally thought that reorganization structures are important tools to avoid excessive and economically disruptive liquidation of firms' assets.[10] And if given a choice of possible approaches to reorganization, the cost of any particular system, weighed against its benefits, provides an obvious metric for evaluation.

In this context, a study of the costs of chapter 11 of the United States Bankruptcy Code is important along at least two dimensions. First, such a study is important within the United States, as it provides important information for policymakers and creditors about the efficiency of the present system and how it might compare with possible alternatives.[11] Second, and perhaps more importantly, given the economic relevance of the United States, which remains the largest single economy, and its relatively long history of corporate reorganization,[12] the cost of chapter 11 can provide important information in other jurisdictions seeking to remodel their own business bankruptcy systems.[13]

This study provides an examination of chapter 11 costs using two datasets. First, I examine a dataset comprised of more than 900 randomly selected chapter 11 cases filed in 2004. In addition, I also utilize a dataset of 97 large chapter 11 cases, also filed in 2004. Both datasets are amongst the largest, if not the largest, datasets ever used in a study of chapter 11 costs. Considered together, these two

8 *See* Douglas G. Baird & Donald S. Bernstein, *Absolute Priority, Valuation Uncertainty, and the Reorganization Bargain*, 115 YALE L.J. 1930 (2006); Lynn M. LoPucki & William C. Whitford, *Bargaining over Equity's Share in the Bankruptcy Reorganization of Large, Publicly Held Companies*, 139 U. PA. L. REV. 125, 126 (1990) ("Current law provides a complex legal environment in which representatives of thousands of creditors and shareholders bargain over the disposition of billions of dollars in assets.")

9 *See, e.g.*, Andrei Shleifer & Robert W. Vishny, *Liquidation Values and Debt Capacity: A Market Equilibrium Approach*, 47 J. FIN. 1343 (1992); Todd C. Pulvino, *Do Asset Fire Sales Exist? An Empirical Investigation of Commercial Aircraft Transactions*, 53 J. FIN. 939 (1998).

10 United States v. Whiting Pools, Inc., 462 U.S. 198, 203 (1983) ("In proceedings under the reorganization provisions of the Bankruptcy Code, a troubled enterprise may be restructured to enable it to operate successfully in the future... . Congress presumed that the assets of the debtor would be more valuable if used in a rehabilitated business than if 'sold for scrap.'"). *See* Frank H. Easterbrook, *Is Corporate Bankruptcy Efficient?*, 27 J. FIN. ECON. 411 (1990); Elizabeth Warren, *Bankruptcy Policymaking in an Imperfect World*, 92 MICH. L. REV. 336 (1993); Elizabeth Warren & Jay L. Westbrook, *Contracting Out of Bankruptcy: An Empirical Intervention*, 118 HARV. L. REV. 1197 (2005).

11 *Cf.* Elizabeth Warren & Jay Lawrence Westbrook, *The Success of Chapter 11: A Challenge to the Critics*, 107 MICH. L. REV. 603, 612-40 (2009).

12 *See generally* Stephen J. Lubben, *Railroad Receiverships and Modern Bankruptcy Theory*, 89 CORNELL L. REV. 1420 (2004) (discussing the early history of American corporate reorganization, which dates back to the second half of the nineteenth century).

13 Jay Lawrence Westbrook, *A Global Solution to Multinational Default*, 98 MICH. L. REV. 2276, 2278-79 nn.2-15 (2000) (detailing bankruptcy reform efforts throughout the world).

datasets provide important insights not only on the very large cases that are the subject of most theoretical inquiry, but also for the more typically smaller chapter 11 cases that might be more comparable with bankruptcy or insolvency cases in other jurisdictions.

Chapter 11 is part of a larger system of American business bankruptcy. The current Bankruptcy Code was enacted in 1978,[14] replacing the prior Bankruptcy Act, which had been in place since 1898, although with substantial amendments enacted during the 1930s.[15] Chapters 1, 3, and 5 provide general provisions that apply in all types of bankruptcy cases, personal and business. Chapter 7 provides the kind of liquidation bankruptcy proceeding that can be found in any developed economy: A trustee takes charge of the debtor's assets, sells them, and pays out the proceeds to creditors according to a set statutory scheme. Chapter 11 can be used for either reorganization or liquidation, but the default rule is that the debtor stays "in possession" of its own bankruptcy estate, with a trustee appointed only in cases of gross mismanagement.

Under both chapters 7 and 11, debtors enjoy the protection of an automatic stay, which prohibits most collection efforts as soon as the bankruptcy petition is filed. And while chapter 11 is often derided as overly long and overly expensive, such simple descriptions of chapter 11 ignore the dynamic nature of the process, which is no longer as it was when first enacted in 1978.[16]

* * *

The aim of this study is on one level descriptive. I describe the nature of chapter 11 costs, and how those costs are distributed in chapter 11 cases. Moreover, I develop models of chapter 11 direct costs that can be used to predict chapter 11 costs *ex ante* and evaluate chapter 11 costs *ex post*.

And the goal of the study is also to provide specific information about the components of chapter 11 cost. In particular, in Chapters 5 and 6 I look at the cost associated with bankruptcy attorneys and financial advisors. Taken together, these two groups of professionals account for almost 60% of total chapter 11 costs.

Another goal of this study is to provide baseline information for considering both the efficiency of chapter 11 and the cost of future chapter 11 cases. The models presented in this paper allow for a prediction of what a typical chapter 11 case should cost. Future cases that fall outside the prediction intervals warrant extra scrutiny and even criticism. And the cost information presented herein provides

14 Bankruptcy Reform Act of 1978, Pub. L. No. 95-598, 92 Stat. 2549 (1978) (effective Oct. 1, 1979). The Bankruptcy Code is codified as title 11 of the United States Code. 11 U.S.C. §§ 101-1330. Chapter 11 is one subpart of title 11, which contains the entire Code.

15 Bankruptcy Act of 1898, ch. 541, 30 Stat. 544, amended by the Chandler Act of 1938, ch. 575, 52 Stat. 840 (repealed 1979).

16 David A. Skeel, Jr., *Creditors' Ball: The "New" New Corporate Governance in Chapter 11*, 152 U. Pa. L. Rev. 917, 918 (2003) ("The endless negotiations and mind-numbingly bureaucratic process that seemed to characterize bankruptcy in the 1980s have been replaced by transactions that look more like the market for corporate control.").

a basis for comparing chapter 11 to other American corporate transactions, as well as other corporate reorganization systems, both theoretical and actual systems in use in other jurisdictions.

II Prior Studies

The costs of corporate bankruptcy or reorganization are often considered to encompass two concepts.[17] First, there are the direct costs, comprised chiefly of the professional fees associated with reorganization, but also including other lesser costs like court filing fees and, in the Untied States, quarterly fees due to the United States Trustee's office.[18] In addition, there are also indirect costs of a firm's bankruptcy, which are more abstract but include things like lost revenues, lost opportunities, and lost goodwill. Some of these costs may be of concern to the firm's stakeholders, but not to policymakers if, for example, financial distress simply results in the shifting of sales from the distressed firm to a competitor firm – unless the competitor is abroad.

These indirect costs are not only difficult to measure generally, but it is also difficult to determine what portion of these costs are attributable to any particular bankruptcy system.[19] Firms that fail are likely to incur lost sales and the like even in a jurisdiction without a bankruptcy or insolvency system.[20] The indirect costs of a particular bankruptcy system like chapter 11, as opposed to the indirect costs of financial distress generally, are in truth then the marginal difference in such costs between the system under study and some alternative, often a hypothetical world with no bankruptcy system.[21]

17 As the focus of this study is on chapter 11 costs, this chapter intentionally neglects several important studies of the costs of European or Canadian corporate bankruptcy procedures, including John Armour et al., *Corporate Insolvency In The United Kingdom: The Impact of the Enterprise Act 2002*, 5 EUROPEAN CO. & FIN. L. REV. 135 (2008); Oscar Couwenberg & Abe de Jong, *Costs And Recovery Rates In The Dutch Liquidation-Based Bankruptcy System*, European 26 EUROPEAN J. L. & ECON. 105 (2008); Timothy C. G. Fisher & Jocelyn Martel, *The Irrelevance of Direct Bankruptcy Costs to the Firm's Financial Reorganization Decision*, 2 J. EMP. L. STUD. 151 (2005).

18 The United States Trustee Program is a component of the Department of Justice that monitors bankruptcy cases for fraud and the like. It is distinct from the bankruptcy trustee appointed in all chapter 7 and some chapter 11 cases.

19 Gregor Andrade & Steven N. Kaplan, *How Costly is Financial (Not Economic) Distress? Evidence from Highly Leveraged Transactions that Became Distressed*, 53 J. FIN. 1443 (1998) (finding that most of the indirect cost of financial distress seems to be incurred before bankruptcy).

20 As noted by an earlier commentator in a related context:

There is a common tendency to view bankruptcy as an "either-or" situation. Either the firm is solvent and there are no costs or the firm is bankrupt and there are costs. In fact, for indirect costs, there is usually a continuum of costs that increase at an accelerating rate as exposure to bankruptcy increases . . .

Bernell K. Stone, *Bankruptcy Costs: Some Evidence: Discussion*, 32 J. FIN. 366, 367 (1977). See also R.A. Haugen & L.W. Senbet, *Bankruptcy and Agency Costs: Their Significance to the Theory of Optimal Capital Structure*, 23 J. FIN. & QUANT. ANAL. 27 (1988).

21 Depending on the basis of comparison, the indirect costs could thus be negative.

Although there have been some efforts to study indirect costs empirically,[22] and one recent study suggests that the total expected cost of financial distress may be as high as 4.5% of the firm's pre-distress assets, [23] more often efforts to examine these costs have been theoretical, particularly in the legal literature.[24] In addition, studies of indirect costs have been limited to publicly held companies, and it is unknown if the results found in that context will translate to privately held firms, which make up the vast majority of debtors.

Studies of the direct costs of corporate reorganization date to the Great Depression.[25] Between the 1930s and the enactment of the current United States Bankruptcy Code in 1978, the most important study of direct costs was Jerold Warner's examination of railroads that filed under section 77 of the Bankruptcy Act between 1933 and 1955.[26] Warner's study continues to make occasional appearances in the literature,[27] despite its exceedingly small sample size,[28] focus on an industry that was in many ways atypical of corporate bankruptcy practice under the old Bankruptcy Act,[29] and the use of a sample that was arguably already out of date when published in 1977.

The first significant study of professional fees under chapter 11 was Weiss (1990), who studied a sample of 37 publicly traded firms that filed for bankruptcy

22 Edward I. Altman, *A Further Empirical Investigation of the Bankruptcy Cost Question*, 39 J. FIN. 1067 (1984) (measuring indirect costs by consideration of comparable company sales, but without specifying what portion of said costs are attributable to the bankruptcy system and what portion might be the result of general financial distress.); Andrade & Kaplan, *supra* note 19; T.C. Opler & S. Titman, *Financial Distress and Corporate Performance*, 49 J. FIN. 1015, 1040 (1994).

23 Heitor Almeida & Tomas Philippon, *The Risk-Adjusted Cost of Financial Distress*, 62 J. Fin. 2557 (2007).

24 *E.g.*, Barry E. Adler, *Bankruptcy and Risk Allocation*, 77 CORNELL L. REV. 439 (1992); James J. White, *Harvey's Silence*, 69 AM. BANKR. L.J. 467 (1995).

25 THOMAS CLIFFORD BILLIG, EQUITY RECEIVERSHIPS IN THE COMMON PLEAS COURT OF FRANKLIN COUNTY, OHIO (1932); Israel Treiman, *An Analysis of the Statistical Data on Receivership Suits Filed in the St. Louis Circuit Court 1925-32 Inclusive*, 19 ST. LOUIS L. REV. 87 (1933). *See* Stephen J. Lubben, *Railroad Receiverships and Modern Bankruptcy Theory*, 89 CORNELL L. REV. 1420, 1452 (2004) (noting that one railroad paid attorneys alone more than $900,000 during the reorganization, which represented approximately 3.5% of its pre-receivership assets); *see also* Churchill Rodgers & Litlleton Groom *Reorganization of Railroad Corporations Under Section 77 of the Bankruptcy Act*, 33 COLUM. L. REV. 571, 571 n.2 (1933) (citing Paxton, *Railroad Receiverships and Reorganizations* (1933) 1 Ed. Research Rep., No. 2; Moulton and Associates, The American Transportation Problem (1933) *333 et seq.*; Chicago, M. & St. Paul Reorganization, 131 I.C.C. 673, 699 (1928)) ("The reorganization of the Wabash, 1911-1916 [was] reported to have cost $3,449,500; Pere Marquette, 1912-1917, $2,769,000; Western Pacific, 1915-1916, $2,000,000; Chicago, Milwaukee & St. Paul, 1925-1928, in excess of $5,000,000.").

26 Jerold B. Warner, *Bankruptcy Costs: Some Evidence*, 32 J. FIN. 337 (1977) (finding that professional fees averaged four percent of total assets). There is also some information on bankruptcy costs in the 1960s contained in DAVID T. STANLEY & MARJORIE GIRTH, BANKRUPTCY: PROBLEM, PROCESS, REFORM (1971).

27 Arturo Bris, Alan Schwartz, & Ivo Welch, *Who Should Pay for Bankruptcy Costs?*, 34 J. LEGAL STUD. 295, 296 n.1 (2005).

28 Eleven cases.

29 Only railroads could reorganize under section 77, railroads were not permitted to liquidated, and the railroads' proceedings were subject to oversight by the Interstate Commerce Commission.

between 1979 and 1986.[30] This study found costs to be, on average, 3.1% of the book value of debt plus market value of equity at the end of the fiscal year preceding bankruptcy, which was substantially less than the 4% to 25% that prior studies had reported.[31] Weiss (1990) ultimately concluded that chapter 11 direct costs "will have little or no impact on the pricing of claims prior to bankruptcy."[32]

In 1996, Tashjian and others published a study of prepackaged chapter 11 cases,[33] utilizing a sample of forty-nine firms that filed prepackaged chapter 11 cases between 1986 and the first six months of 1993.[34] The authors found that prepackaged cases fall between out-of-court and chapter 11 restructurings in terms of time, direct costs, recovery rates, and violations of absolute priority. Overall, the authors reported direct costs of 1.85% of assets.

In 1997, Brian Betker studied a sample of 157 firms that experienced financial distress between 1986 and 1993, including 75 traditional chapter 11 cases, 48 prepacks and 29 exchange offers.[35] He found that the direct costs of traditional chapter 11 cases averaged 3.93% of total pre-bankruptcy assets (median 3.37%), which was substantially larger than average direct costs for prepacks (mean 2.85%, median 2.38%), though direct costs for prepacks were not significantly larger than those for exchange offers (mean 2.51%, median 1.98%).[36] Betker further found evidence of economies of scale in restructuring debt, that is direct costs increased with total assets but declined with the square of total assets and that the restructuring type did not effect the "concave relation between direct costs and

30 Lawrence A. Weiss, *Bankruptcy Resolution: Direct Costs and Violation of Priority of Claims*, 27 J. Fin. Econ. 285 (1990). There were other studies of bankruptcy costs between 1978 and 1990, but often these papers used multi-year samples that failed to note the enactment of a new Bankruptcy Code in 1978, or assumed, sometimes only implicitly, that cases filed under the old Bankruptcy Act were relevant to determining the cost structure of cases under the new Code. *See, e.g.*, S. Ang et al., *Administrative Costs Of Corporate Bankruptcy: A Note*, 37 J. Fin. 219 (1989) (studying cases from before the enactment of the 1978 Bankruptcy Code).

31 *Id.* at 286.

32 *Id.* at 299.

33 As explained in Lubben (2000), *infra*:

A true prepack involves a prepetition solicitation of votes on a plan. A partial prepack involves both a prepetition solicitation (e.g., of bondholders) and a postpetition solicitation (e.g., of equity). Partial prepacks are usually done to avoid having to conduct a "registered prepack," which is subject to review and comment by the SEC, and takes substantially longer than a non-registered prepack. A prearranged or prenegotiated case involves no prepetition solicitation, and thus is little different from a traditional Chapter 11 case, save for the fact that a proposed plan and disclosure statement are fully drafted on the first day of the case. (footnotes omitted).

34 Elizabeth Tashjian et al., *Pre-Packs: An Empirical Analysis of Prepackaged Bankruptcies*, 40 J. Fin. Econ. 135 (1996). As noted in Lubben (2000), *infra*, the definition of "prepackaged" used in this paper likely also includes prenegotiated chapter 11 cases.

35 Brian L. Betker, *The Administrative Costs of Debt Restructurings: Some Recent Evidence*, 26 Fin. Mgmt. 56 (1997) (hereinafter "Betker (1997)"). Betker defined a prepack as "one in which the firm filed both a bankruptcy petition and plan at the same time and where the firm's creditors had either officially accepted the plan in a binding vote or all impaired creditor classes agreed in principle to vote for the plan" and an exchange offer as "an out-of-court restructuring in which new securities (cash, equity, or debt) are exchanged for old debt." *Id.* at 58.

36 *Id.* at 57.

firm size."[37] Betker found that median cost for traditional chapter 11s was 4.63% of total post-restructuring assets plus cash and property distributed to creditors, which was significantly larger than that for prepacks (2.64%) or exchange offers (2.26%).[38] Thus, Betker concluded that firms involved in chapter 11 reorganizations lost more value than firms involved in prepacks or exchange offers.[39]

In an attempt to understand the varying levels of direct costs, Betker related direct costs as a percentage of pre-restructuring total assets to a series of explanatory variables.[40] He found that on average, traditional chapter 11 cases were larger than prepacks or exchange offers, though the median firm size did not differ significantly.[41] Prepacks were more likely to involve leveraged buyouts than chapter 11 cases or exchange offers.[42] Exchange offers tended to restructure the smallest fraction of debt while chapter 11 cases restructured the most classes of debt.[43] Further, traditional chapter 11 was typically used to restructure private and trade debt, while prepacks and exchange offers were mostly used to restructure public debt.[44] Finally "vulture" or distressed investors ended up with equity blocks in 44 cases.[45]

Betker found that the study's results for traditional chapter 11 cases were consistent with his expectations.[46] The ratio of direct costs to assets was lower in cases involving leveraged buyouts, but the cost savings declined as the fraction of public debt in the capital structure increased.[47] Debtors incurred less direct costs when a vulture investor acquired a 5% stake in the reorganized debtor, but those cost savings decreased as the firm size increased.[48] For prepacks, Betker concluded that direct costs were negatively related to firm size and positively related to the proportion of restructured debt held by trade creditors.[49] So-called "vulture" involvement did not seem to significantly effect the costs of prepacks.[50] For exchange offers, the results indicated that direct costs were positively related

37 *Id.* at 59. The question of whether chapter 11 cost is subject to "economies of scale" has been the subject of dueling definitions, and this author is guilty of using both definitions. Betker, Lawless, and Lubben (2000) defined economies of scale as a non-linear relationship between size and cost, while LoPucki and Lubben (2008) suggest a definition that means cost increases on less than a one for one basis with size – i.e., the slope of the relationship is less than one. This study uses the former definition.

38 *Id.* at 61.

39 *Id.* at 61.

40 *Id.*

41 *Id.* at 63.

42 *Id.*

43 *Id.*

44 *Id.* at 63. For example, none of the 29 exchange offers and only 10 of the 48 prepacks restructured any trade debt while only 9 of the 29 exchange offers restructured any private debt. *Id.*

45 *Id.* at 64.

46 *Id.*

47 *Id.* at 66.

48 *Id.*

49 *Id.*

50 *Id.* at 66.

to the percentage of debt and the number of classes restructured and negatively related to firm size.[51]

Betker ultimately concluded that prepackaged bankruptcy costs were similar to exchange offers, and both were lower than traditional chapter 11 filings.[52] Direct costs in chapter 11 cases were lower if the firm involved was a leveraged buyout, but the cost savings decreased as the ratio of public debt to total debt increased.[53] Direct costs of chapter 11 were also lower when vulture investors were involved in the restructuring.[54] In short, Betker's study indicated that debt restructurings were less expensive when creditors had less trouble coordinating their efforts.[55]

More recently, this author set out to consider assertions that direct costs of chapter 11 were "excessive."[56] I conducted a study of 22 corporate bankruptcies and reported evidence that the direct costs of chapter 11 were in fact nominal, both empirically and analytically, that is, "not only on a simple percentage basis but also in relation to other significant corporate transactions."[57]

The study examined professional fees along three dimensions: "(a) fees as a percentage of the firm's overall debt load, (b) fees as a percentage of the debtor's reported assets, and (c) fees in relation to total firm size."[58] With respect to the entire sample, the direct costs of chapter 11 were found to average 0.87% of total firm size (assets plus debts).[59] When prepackaged bankruptcies were removed from the sample, the direct costs increased to 1.20% of total firm size.[60] When measured as a percentage of assets, direct costs were found to average 1.8% for the entire sample and 2.5% when prepacks were excluded.[61] I ultimately concluded that "the direct costs of the current Chapter 11 regime are quite modest, and [thus] the efficiency gains from many of the proposed reforms may be quite feeble, if such gains are not lacking altogether."[62]

Lubben (2000) turned out to be the opening act in a multitude of empirical legal studies of business bankruptcy costs over the next decade. That same year, Lawless and Ferris reported on their study of small business chapter 11 costs.[63]

51 *Id.*
52 *Id.* at 56.
53 *Id.*
54 *Id.*
55 *Id.* at 67.
56 Stephen J. Lubben, *The Direct Costs of Corporate Reorganization: An Empirical Examination of Professional Fees in Large Chapter 11 Cases*, 74 AM. BANKR. L.J. 509, 510 (2000) (hereinafter "Lubben (2000)") (citing SOL STEIN, A FEAST FOR LAWYERS: INSIDE CHAPTER 11 – AN EXPOSE (1989); Lynn M. LoPucki, *The Trouble with Chapter 11*, 1993 WIS. L. REV. 729 n.6; Alexander L. Paskay & Frances Pilaro Wolstenholme, *Chapter 11: A Growing Cash Cow Some Thoughts on How to Rein in the System*, 1 AM. BANKR. INST. L. REV. 331 (1993)).
57 Lubben (2000), *supra* note 51, at 511.
58 *Id.* at 512.
59 *Id.*
60 *Id.* at 512-13.
61 *Id.* at 513.
62 *Id.*
63 Stephen P. Ferris & Robert M. Lawless, *The Expenses of Financial Distress: The Direct Costs of Chapter 11*, 61 U. PITT. L. REV. 629 (2000). The authors had previously studied small business

Studying multiple judicial districts, the authors reported median costs of 3.5% of debtor assets. The authors concluded that whether "measured by total distributions or total assets, chapter 11 costs are of a relatively low magnitude and at a level consistent with studies of large corporate bankruptcies." [64]

In 2004, Lynn LoPucki and Joseph Doherty reported on "one of the most extensive studies to date of the professional fees and expenses awarded by U.S. bankruptcy courts in the reorganization of large, public companies."[65] LoPucki and Doherty studied the professional fees and expenses awarded by U.S. bankruptcy courts in 48 chapter 11 cases involving large, public companies whose plans were confirmed between 1998 and 2002.[66]

The authors constructed a regression model of the principal determinants of fees and expenses applied for and awarded to the professionals involved in the sample's reorganizations in order to test the impact of different variables on such awards.[67] They tested a number of different variables, including the size of the firm, the length of the case, the court of the bankruptcy proceeding, the number of professional firms involved in the case, the solvency of the firm, the type of reorganization plan being confirmed, the firm's industry, the amount of fee cuts imposed by the court, whether the firm was liquidated during the bankruptcy proceeding, whether the debtor's lawyers were from New York, whether the firm ultimately liquidated or reorganized, and whether the debtor's lawyers were local to the court.[68] However, LoPucki and Doherty ultimately settled on just four variables for use in their regression: firm size (measured by the assets reported on the bankruptcy petition), case duration, the number of professional firms seeking fees and the location of the bankruptcy proceeding.[69]

Using this model, LoPucki and Doherty concluded that firm size and length of time between filing and confirmation were the strongest determinants of professional fees awarded.[70] Further, the number of professional firms seeking reimbursement also impacted the overall amount of professional fees awarded, albeit causing a smaller effect than the first two variables.[71] Using only those three factors in their regression analysis, LoPucki and Doherty were able to explain 77% of the variance of fees.[72] Additionally, by controlling for those three variables, the

chapter 7 costs. Robert M. Lawless & Stephen P. Ferris, *Professional Fees and Other Direct Costs in Chapter 7 Business Liquidations*, 75 WASH. U. L.Q. 1207 (1997). *See also* Robert M. Lawless et al., *A Glimpse at Professional Fees and Other Direct Costs in Small Firm Bankruptcies*, 1994 U. ILL. L. REV. 847.

64 Ferris & Lawless (2000), *supra* note 63, at 651.

65 Lynn M. LoPucki & Joseph W. Doherty, *The Determination of Professional Fees in Large Bankruptcy Reorganization Cases*, 1 J. EMP. L. STUD. 111, 111 (2004).

66 *Id.*

67 LoPucki & Doherty, *supra* note 65, at 119.

68 *Id.* at 119-20.

69 *Id.* at 120.

70 *Id.*

71 *Id.* at 120.

72 *Id.*

authors found that fees were significantly higher for bankruptcy cases proceeding in Delaware – approximately 32% higher.[73]

Shortly thereafter, this author published a two-part article looking at the internal mechanics of attorney fees in chapter 11.[74] Using the billing records of a large corporate law firm in a single Delaware chapter 11 case, I demonstrated that more than 60% of the attorneys were not bankruptcy specialists, suggesting that a good deal of the costs that appear on fee applications may be exogenous to the chapter 11 process. Since this data suggests that the direct costs of chapter 11 itself might be even lower than previously reported, I concluded by noting the challenge that this presented for those who argue that chapter 11 has a substantial effect on *ex ante* debt prices. Once discounted by the probability of default and time until such default, such small amounts would only be important in highly efficient markets, of which the debt markets are unlikely examples.

Moreover, I also noted that the data showed that most of the cost of chapter 11 was attributable to the mid-range attorneys, neither the most expensive nor the most junior attorneys that were often the focus of courts and the press.

In 2006, Bris, Welch and Zhu published a study of almost 300 corporate bankruptcies filed in Arizona and New York from 1995-2001.[75] The sample was comprised of 225 chapter 11 cases and 61 chapter 7 cases. The authors note problems with missing data that also appear in the present study, and any study that attempts to move beyond the very large publicly traded debtors covered by commercial data services:

> All data are hand coded from the full bankruptcy documents. Although the forms are standardized, each firm reported its information in a different format. Some firms did not even report basic data, such as assets, despite a legal requirement to do so. In some cases, we have no choice but to discard the entire observation. In other cases, we can use an observation in some tests, but not in others.

The authors found that the average time spent in chapter 7 is 1.9 years, and the average time spent in chapter 11 is 2.3 years. They further concluded that that chapter 7 liquidations are no faster or cheaper than chapter 11 reorganizations, once differences in firm characteristics were accounted for. As with the LoPucki (2004) and Lubben (2008)[76] studies, the authors found that courts rarely deny fee applications. They also noted that bankruptcy costs are highly sensitive to the size of debtor being measured and how size itself is measured, both in terms of which metric is used (assets, debts, etc.) and the source of the data used.

73 LoPucki & Doherty, *supra* note 65, at 120-21.

74 Stephen J. Lubben, *The Microeconomics of Chapter 11*, Part 2, 4 INT'L. CORP. RESCUE 87 (2007); *The Microeconomics of Chapter 11*, Part 1, 4 INT'L. CORP. RESCUE 31 (2007).

75 Bris, Welch & Zhu, *The Costs of Bankruptcy: Chapter 7 Liquidation Versus Chapter 11 Reorganization*, 61 J FIN. 1 253 (2006).

76 *Infra.*

2008 then saw the publication of three major empirical legal studies of chapter 11 costs. First, LoPucki and Doherty returned to their original model and compared it with a new model, that they asserted better represented pure case complexity.[77] Describing the difference between the two regression models as the "billing opportunity" presented by a case, the authors asserted that professionals routinely overcharged for chapter 11 work.

Next, this author produced the American Bankruptcy Institute Chapter 11 Fee Study,[78] and published a related article setting forth the results of that study.[79] The study examined a total sample of 1,026 cases filed in 2004 as 945 chapter 11 cases were pooled into a "random" sample and 99 cases were considered in a "big case" dataset. The average firm in the big case dataset had scheduled assets of $423.4 million and scheduled liabilities of nearly $776 million, while the average firm in the random sample had scheduled assets of $21.2 million and scheduled liabilities of more than $37 million. Lubben (2008) found that for both samples professional fees totaled 4 to 4.5 percent of the bankrupt firms' assets and liabilities, but cautioned against reporting cost in relation to size, since the data evidenced significant economics of scale.

While partially confirming prior studies, such as LoPucki and Doherty (2004), Lubben (2008) also found that time spent in chapter 11 was not a significant predictor of overall cost once case complexity was directly modeled. Lubben (2008) found the addition of other variables, such the presence of official committees and whether there were "first day motions" filed in a case, were better predictors of the costs involved in a chapter 11 case. The study also found no indications that filing in Delaware or New York resulted in greater cost.

Also in 2008, LoPucki and Doherty examined the growing role of investment bankers in modern chapter 11 practice and constructed regression models for specific bankruptcy professionals.[80] The primary findings of this paper largely track those of its earlier companion papers, although the authors did note that "the fees of financial advisors grew at the rate of 25% per year, as compared with an increase in all professional fees and expenses of 7% per year." They also separately modeled the costs of lead debtor's attorneys, finding that Skadden, Arps, a leading New York corporate law firm,[81] was substantially more expensive than other debtors' firms. They concluded "Skadden Arps representation cost more in these cases because Skadden Arps billed more hours."

77 Lynn M. LoPucki & Joseph W. Doherty, *Professional Overcharging in Large Bankruptcy Reorganization Cases*, 5 J. Empirical L. Stud. 983 (2008).

78 The ABI Chapter 11 Fee Study is available online (http://ssrn.com/abstract=1020477).

79 Stephen J. Lubben, *Corporate Reorganization & Professional Fees*, 82 Am. Bankr. L.J. 77 (2008) (hereinafter, "Lubben (2008)").

80 Lynn M. LoPucki and Joseph W. Doherty, *Rise of the Financial Advisors: An Empirical Study of the Division of Professional Fees in Large Bankruptcies*, 82 Am. Bankr. L. J. 141 (2008).

81 Skadden, Arps, Slate, Meagher & Flom LLP.

Summary

The leading studies of the costs of corporate reorganization are from prior generations, and are now quite out of date. Warner studied cases that were already old when his study was published in 1977, and Weiss's 1990 study, while a vast improvement, involves cases from a different era in chapter 11 practice.

More recent studies by Lubben, Lawless and LoPucki improve and update these prior studies, but still suffer from their own problems. Lawless studies very small chapter 11 cases. LoPucki's make strong claims about chapter 11 cost based on small samples, which stretch over several years. Lubben's 2008 study was limited to a two-year view of chapter 11 cost.

In short, the costs of chapter 11 have been heavily studied, but in a largely piecemeal and incremental manner. Large and small cases have been the subject of distinct studies, but rarely have the two been studied across comparable datasets. This study presents a unified picture of the whole of chapter 11.

III The Datasets

I begin with the data I collected for the American Bankruptcy Institute's Chapter 11 Fee Study.[82] The ABI Chapter 11 Fee Study database is comprised of two sub-datasets, a random sample and a "big case" dataset. Both datasets include cases that were originally filed in 2004, and the data within each dataset comes from publicly available court filings that were primarily collected from PACER.[83]

The United States has both federal and state-level court systems. Because the United States Constitution gives the federal Congress the power to pass "uniform Laws on the subject of Bankruptcies throughout the United States," the present study considers only the federal court system.[84] There are 94 federal judicial districts throughout the United States, including at least one district in each state, plus the District of Columbia and Puerto Rico.[85] States with large populations have multiple districts – for example, New York, Texas and California each have four judicial districts.[86] Smaller population states, like New Hampshire and Utah, consist of a single district. The bankruptcy courts are units of the district courts, and thus there is a bankruptcy court within each judicial district in the United States, although they typically hear cases in a distinct bankruptcy courthouse.

These 94 districts are organized into 12 regional circuits, each of which has a United States Court of Appeals. The United States Court of Appeals for the District of Columbia is the federal appellate court for the U.S. District Court for the District of Columbia and certain administrative agencies. All other circuits are numbered one through 11 and cover at least three states, and the Courts of Appeal for those circuits hear appeals from the district and bankruptcy courts therein.[87]

The random sample was drawn from 33 judicial districts around the United States. Three districts from each of the eleven numbered judicial circuits were selected: one from each of the high, low and median population states in the circuit, as determined by the July 1, 2003 Population Estimate published by the U.S.

82 The ABI Chapter 11 Fee Study is available online (http://ssrn.com/abstract=1020477) and is extensively discussed in Stephen J. Lubben, *Corporate Reorganization & Professional Fees*, 82 AM. BANKR. L.J. 77 (2008) (hereinafter, "Lubben (2008)").

83 http://pacer.psc.uscourts.gov/. *See generally*, Jay Lawrence Westbrook, *Empirical Research in Consumer Bankruptcy*, 80 TEX. L. REV. 2123, 2148 (2002).

84 U.S. CONST. art. I, § 8, cl. 4 (providing Congress has power "[t]o establish an uniform Rule of Naturalization, and uniform Laws on the subject of Bankruptcies throughout the United States . . .").

85 Three territories of the United States – the Virgin Islands, Guam, and the Northern Mariana Islands – also have district courts that hear federal cases.

86 http://www.uscourts.gov/images/CircuitMap.pdf.

87 Bankruptcy appeals first go to either the District Court or a Bankruptcy Appellate Panel (comprised of three bankruptcy judges from within the circuit but outside of the district) and then to the Courts of Appeal, with discretionary review by the United States Supreme Court.

Census. In states with multiple districts, the district that included the highest population city was chosen.

For example, California was chosen as the high population state from the 9th Circuit, and the Central District of California, which includes Los Angeles, was selected as the California district for inclusion in the sample. Where there was an even number of states in the circuit, I calculated the average population for the circuit and selected the state with the population closest to that figure as the "median population state." Cases had an equal chance of selection regardless of the location within the district where they were filed. For example, cases from the Southern District of New York include cases filed in both the Manhattan and White Plains courthouses.

As a result of the destruction caused by Hurricane Katrina in late August 2005, neighboring districts replaced two districts originally included in the sample. In particular, the Northern District of Mississippi was substituted for the Southern District and the Western District of Louisiana was substituted for the Eastern District. These changes were made both to avoid the need to work with courts whose operations were tremendously disrupted by the storm and to avoid any skewing effects on the sample that the devastation in these two districts might have had. Of course, the replacement districts neighbored the areas of greatest destruction, but for purposes of comparability, I felt it important to use replacement districts that were within the same state as the original districts, to ensure the same background debtor-creditor law.

Up to forty cases were selected from each district. Up to twenty cases were selected from the first six months of 2004, and up to twenty more cases were selected from the final half of the year.

Within each six-month period, cases were selected in the order they were filed. Only business entities were included in the sample; cases involving individual debtors were passed over as part of the selection process. A series of related cases, filed together, was counted only as a single case, with the lead (or first-filed, if there was no lead) case included in the database.

The big case dataset is non-random, comprising all 2004 bankruptcy cases listed in the "Major Bankruptcies" database on www.bankruptcydata.com (published by New Generation Research, Inc.) except for cases initially filed under chapter 7 and not converted to chapter 11 and cases filed under the former section 304 of the Bankruptcy Code.[88]

Within these two datasets, the author and his research assistants reviewed the court dockets for each case and selected pleadings for inclusion in the database. Law firms throughout the United States provided electronic copies of the requested documents. The author and his research assistants then hand-coded the two datasets.

88 Section 304 was repealed in 2005 as part of the enactment of new chapter 15. Both section 304 and the new chapter 15 deal with the recognition of foreign bankruptcy proceedings in the United States. *See* Jay Lawrence Westbrook, *Chapter 15 at Last*, 79 AM. BANKR. L. J. 713 (2005).

Two broad types of professional fee data were collected in each dataset: debtor professional expenses and committee professional expenses. In particular, under section 330 of the Bankruptcy Code, all professionals retained by either the debtor or an official committee, most often a creditors committee, must file fee applications with the court before they can be paid from estate funds.[89] A similar rule applies to professionals retained by examiners or trustees, and the datasets also include that information. Bankruptcy-related professional fees incurred in the days just before the bankruptcy filing are reported on the debtor's statement of financial affairs and thus also are included in the present study. Professional fees incurred by creditors who have a contractual right to charge such fees to the debtor – such as secured lenders – were not included in this study, inasmuch as these sorts of reimbursement obligations are not subject to section 330 and are therefore not subject to express disclosure.

The datasets also include a wealth of related information about the debtors' cases: more than 700 variables were coded in each case.

* * *

The present study modifies the original ABI datasets in several key respects, particularly with regard to the big case dataset. For example, in the original study cases were followed for two years or until they ceased to be in chapter 11 because either a plan was confirmed, the case was converted to chapter 7, or the case was dismissed.[90] This approach to the data was necessitated by the required timeline for producing the final report under the ABI Chapter 11 Fee Study.

To examine whether this censoring had any effects on the data, I revisited the cases in the big case dataset that were still pending in chapter 11 when the original study was completed and recoded them to include their final resolution and all professional expenses incurred through that resolution.[91]

Additionally, I revamped my approach to measuring the debtor's assets and liabilities in the big case dataset.[92] First, asset and liability information was taken from Bloomberg.[93] Typically this information comes from the most recent pre-bankruptcy SEC filings, but Bloomberg also provides financial information for certain larger privately held companies in the sample (e.g., Tower Records).[94] Then, only if financial information on the debtor was unavailable on Bloomberg,

89 11 U.S.C. §330.

90 The study captured professional fees incurred during the study period, even if approved or requested outside of the study period.

91 Although some cases remained pending in the random sample, the relative effect of pending cases was greater in the big case dataset.

92 In the random dataset, I continue to rely on the debtor's schedules, as the majority of these firms are not covered by Bloomberg.

93 Specifically, using the "FA" function on Bloomberg Professional.

94 73.2% of the cases in the dataset are coded with Bloomberg information.

assets and liability information was taken from the debtor's schedules.[95] This change was done for a variety of reasons, most notably to reduce the risk that debtor size – a key factor in this study – would be miss-specified for the corporate groups in the dataset, since schedules are often filed on a corporation by corporation basis, whereas chapter 11 costs are typically incurred by the group as a whole.

In addition, as is often the case with observational studies of American court proceedings, both datasets suffer from missing data.[96] In general, data is missing either because an anticipated pleading was never filed or because the document in question was never imaged for the PACER system.[97] Data that was never filed, obviously is unobtainable, and given the geographic size of the United States, physically visiting each of the courthouses in the study – in many cases several courthouses in each of the 33 districts studied – was not a realistic option.[98] Such cases are used to the extent they have available data.

Finally, to account for the method of case selection, which may overemphasize cases from small population districts, cases in the random dataset are weighted. For example, in some smaller districts, the random dataset likely includes all eligible chapter 11 cases filed in 2004, and many of these districts saw less than 40 chapter 11 cases that year. On the other hand, in districts like the Central District of California (Los Angeles) and the Southern District of New York (Manhattan) the dataset includes but 40 of the several thousand cases filed in these districts in 2004. To account for this, cases in the random dataset are weighted by the average number of business cases in a district between 2003-2005 period, divided by the number of cases from that district that were included in the dataset.[99] Weighting by the three-year average is done to guard against single year variations in particular districts.

As shown in Figure 1A, weighting the data increases the importance of the 40 cases from New York, while downgrading the relative importance of cases from smaller districts. Each case from New York represents more than six cases, once the weighting is applied.

95 As a general matter, these smaller cases should be less likely to involve multiple entities, and thus less likely to implicate the problems of consolidated or unconsolidated balance sheets and schedules.

96 Lubben (2008), *supra* note 82, contains an extensive discussion of the missing data issues.

97 Although the PACER system was to have been completely operational in all bankruptcy cases filed in 2004, I found several districts (including the E.D. Mich., S.D. Fla., and the N.D. Cal) where the imaging of documents was incomplete.

98 Private firms are available to collect the documents, but retrieving a single case in the big case dataset cost more than $2,000.

99 When weighted, the 944 cases in the random dataset approximate 773.7 cases. The weighted number is less than 944 because cases from small districts are overrepresented in the sample and thus weighted at less than one per case.

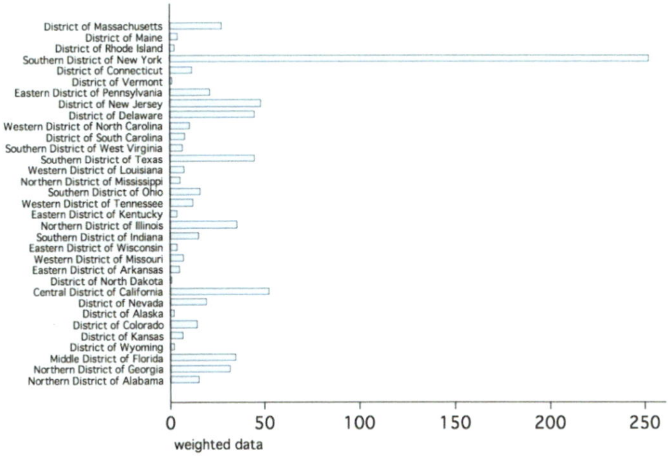

Figure 1A: Case Frequencies by District (Random Sample)

The Administrative Office of the U.S. Courts data used for the weighting calculations is based on total cases filed in the district. When used in the weighting, this method of counting probably results in some extra emphasis on cases from jurisdictions that are especially likely to see large, multi-debtor cases – in particular, the Southern District of New York – since a related group of cases would be considered but one case in my datasets. Regrettably, the Administrative Office does not indicate which cases filed in a district relate to a single corporate group.

Following these changes to the datasets, the big case dataset is comprised of 97 chapter 11 cases, and the random sample dataset includes 944 chapter 11 cases, all filed in 2004. As Figure 1A shows, the random sample is dominated by cases from the Southern District of New York, a jurisdiction that contains not only the largest city in the United States, but also a bankruptcy court that is attractive to business debtors.[100] By contrast, the Central District of California, which contains the nation's second largest city, has much less than half the number of cases. No doubt this reflects the loose correlation between state population size and the number of business bankruptcy cases filed therein, as many businesses may have a choice of jurisdictions in which to file. Figure 1B shows the judicial districts that were sampled in the random dataset overlaid on a map of all districts in the United States.

100 Robert K. Rasmussen & Randall S. Thomas, *Timing Matters: Promoting Forum Shopping by Insolvent Corporations*, 94 Nw. U. L. Rev. 1357, 1360 (2000) (observing that publically traded companies prefer to file chapter 11 in New York and Delaware).

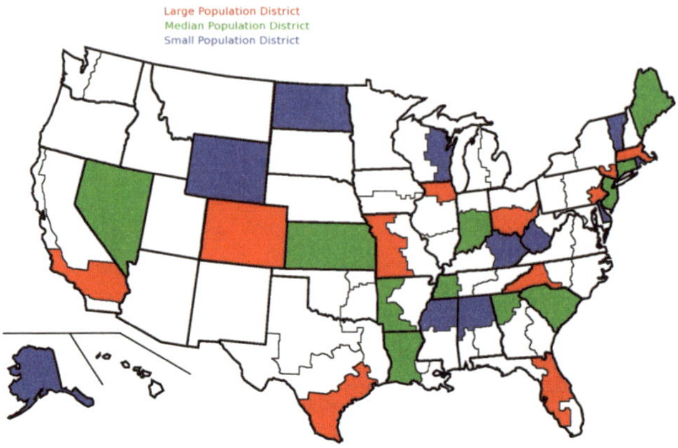

Figure 1B: Judicial Districts in Random Dataset

Table 1C reveals that Delaware and New York are the most prevalent jurisdictions in the big case sample, each representing approximately 14% of the dataset.[101]

Table 1C: Case Frequencies by District (Big Case Dataset)

District	*Freq*	*Plot of freq.*
C.D. Cal.	4	****
Colorado	1	*
D. Ariz.	1	*
D. Del.	13	*************
D. Mass.	2	**
D. Me.	1	*
D. Minn.	1	*
D. Nev.	1	*
D. Vt.	1	*
D. N.H.	1	*
D. N.J.	3	***
E.D. La.	1	*
E.D. Mich.	3	***
E.D. Mo.	1	*
E.D. Tex.	1	*
E.D. Va.	1	*
E.D. Wash.	1	*
M.D. Pa.	1	*

101 In this study all data analysis was done using Stata64/SE version 10.1 for OSX. Stata's survey functions were frequently used in connection with the random sample to ensure appropriate standard errors that reflect the results of the weighting.

Table 1C (continued)

District	*Freq*	*Plot of freq.*
M.D. Florida	3	***
N.D. Cal.	3	***
N.D. Tex.	4	****
N.D. N.Y.	1	*
N.D. Alabama	1	*
N.D. Georgia	3	***
N.D. Illinois	4	****
S.D. Fla.	5	*****
S.D. Ind.	2	**
S.D. N.Y.	14	**************
S.D. Ohio	4	****
S.D. Texas	3	***
W.D. La	4	****
W.D. Pa.	1	*
W.D. Tex.	2	**
W.D. Va.	1	*
W.D. Wash.	1	*
W.D. N.Y.	1	*
W.D. Missouri	2	**
	97	

A. Descriptive Statistics

Figure 2A illustrates the basic financial characteristics of the debtors in the random and big case datasets.[102] As shown, the random dataset, which represents the "typical" chapter 11 case, is comprised of substantially smaller debtors.

In Figure 2A, and many of the figures that follow, the data has been transformed using a log base 10 transformation. This is done to account for the extreme skew of the underlying data, which would otherwise make many of the graphs unusable.[103] The logged numbers are easily interpreted as 1 followed by the number of zeros in the logged value – so that "6" in Figure 2A is the equivalent of $1,000,000. That is, "1" followed by six zeros.

102 Operating income is taken from question 1 of the debtor's Statement of Financial Affairs, which requires the debtor to report "the gross amount of income the debtor has received . . . from operation of the debtor's business." http://www.uscourts.gov/bankform/form7.pdf. The phrasing of this question is somewhat ambiguous, and might lead to inclusion of something more than operating income. For example, if the emphasis is on "received," the debtor might report all sales proceeds or revenues in this field, without deducting the cost of such sales.

103 *See, infra*, Figure 9.

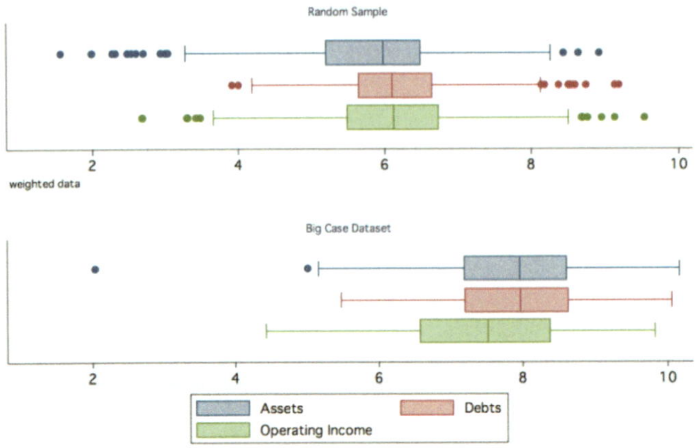

Figure 2A: Financial Characteristics of Debtors (variables log transformed)

Table 2B sets forth descriptive statistics for the two datasets. In both datasets, the prototypical case is one filed by the debtor. Involuntary cases account for about 2% of all cases in both datasets. The cases in the big case dataset are, on average, solvent, while the random sample dataset cases are, on average, heavily insolvent. This highlights a relatively unique aspect of chapter 11 – there is no formal solvency requirement to file a case, and simple cash flow problems or anticipated insolvency can be enough to justify a petition.

But in most respects the two datasets are quite distinct. For example, less than 12% of the cases in the random dataset are publicly traded, whereas more than 55% of the cases in the big case dataset are publicly traded firms required to file reports with the Securities and Exchange Commission.

Big cases are much more likely to involve creditors committees – 77% had at least one committee – while there were committees in less than a quarter of the random sample cases. And while about 27% of the big cases involved sales of most of the debtor's assets, typically before confirmation of a plan, just 6% of the cases in the random dataset involved such sales.[104] Similarly, while the average big debtor saw more than 236 claims filed against it, creditors only filed, on average, 42 claims in the random dataset cases. This in turn leads to the retention of a claims agent in 51% of the big dataset cases, while all but 8% of the random sample debtors rely on the bankruptcy court to manage the claims register.[105]

104 These quick "363 sales," named after the relevant section of the Bankruptcy Code, were recently the subject of much controversy when used by General Motors and Chrysler, but the present datasets show that 363 sales are very much a big case phenomenon.

105 A claims agent is a data-management company that takes over the job of receiving and organizing claims filed in a chapter 11 case. Often a large debtor will want such an agent, as they can

Table 2B: Descriptive Statistics

	Random Dataset (weighted)				Big Case Dataset			
	Mean	*SE of mean*	*Median*	*N*	*Mean*	*SE of mean*	*Median*	*N*
Assets (000s)	$15,700.0	$6,874.2	$810.0	631.8	$706,000.0	$213,000.0	$91,700.0	94
Debts (000s)	$27,600.0	$12,100.0	$1,220.7	626.5	$623,000.0	$170,000.0	$80,000.0	94
Op. In. (000s)	$15,700.0	$4,426.4	$575.5	597.0	$242,000.0	$102,000.0	$7,573.3	77
Publicly Traded	0.12	0.03	0.00	773.7	0.57	0.05	1.00	97
Involuntary	0.02	0.00	0.00	773.7	0.02	0.02	0.00	97
Prepackaged	0.00	0.00	0.00	773.7	0.04	0.02	0.00	97
DIP Loan	0.15	0.04	0.00	773.7	0.43	0.05	0.00	97
# Lawsuits	341.77	344.54	1.00	611.7	52.64	21.44	9.00	74
Trustee	0.07	0.01	0.00	773.7	0.08	0.03	0.00	97
Examiner	0.02	0.01	0.00	773.7	0.06	0.03	0.00	97
Monthly Comp.	0.14	0.05	0.00	773.7	0.47	0.05	0.00	97
Ord. C. Prof.	0.05	0.02	0.00	773.7	0.40	0.05	0.00	97
Claims Agent	0.08	0.04	0.00	773.7	0.47	0.05	0.00	97
363 Motion	0.06	0.02	0.00	773.7	0.27	0.05	0.00	97
Committee	0.24	0.05	0.00	773.7	0.77	0.04	1.00	97
Plan Filed	0.39	0.04	0.00	773.7	0.76	0.04	1.00	97
# Classes	6.47	0.24	6.00	207.2	8.78	0.86	8.00	58
Sub-debt Class	0.04	0.02	0.00	217.7	0.29	0.06	0.00	55
Exit Fin.	0.11	0.05	0.00	208.4	0.20	0.06	0.00	54
Fraud	0.06	0.01	0.00	773.7	0.09	0.03	0.00	97
# Claims	41.56	5.58	13.00	633.8	236.71	120.01	44.00	78
First Day	0.22	0.05	0.00	773.7	0.52	0.05	1.00	97
# Stay Motions	1.35	0.16	1.00	713.7	1.79	0.30	1.00	85
# C/D Motions	0.95	0.06	1.00	730.4	0.63	0.10	0.00	87
# Trustee	0.25	0.07	0.00	696.1	0.50	0.12	0.00	88
Ret. Bonus	0.03	0.01	0.00	773.7	0.36	0.05	0.00	97
3+ Extra Profs.	0.11	0.02	0.00	773.7	0.60	0.05	1.00	97
Fin. Adv.	0.12	0.03	0.00	773.7	0.59	0.05	1.00	97
Days in Ch 11	282.29	9.30	237.00	699.4	410.86	33.63	317.00	97

More information on the variables can be found in Appendix 2B, at the end of the chapter; variance in number of cases reflects (a) missing data and (b) weighting of cases in the random dataset.

These differences carry over into the ways in which the chapter 11 process unfolded in these cases. In the big cases, more than 43% of debtors utilized post-bankruptcy ("DIP") financing, whereas just over 14% of the random sample cases had the benefit of this additional liquidity. Similarly, 40% of the big debtors sought court authorization to pay certain non-bankruptcy professionals outside of the

provide more sophisticated analysis of the claims, and have the facilities to integrate the claims management process with the debtor's financial reports as well as the claims objections process. The debtor pays the expense of hiring such a firm.

normal bankruptcy process, while only 5% of random sample debtors sought similar accommodations.[106]

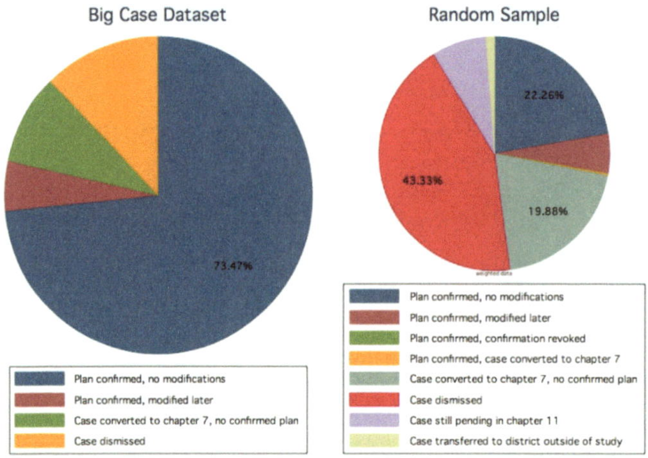

Figure 3: Case Outcomes

The typical big case dataset debtor took just over 410 days (1.13 years) to travel through chapter 11, while cases in the random dataset took, on average, just over 282 days (0.77 years).[107] As shown in Figure 3, these differing times are reflective of very different outcomes in the two datasets. In short, confirmed plans are much more common among the bigger cases, while the random dataset debtors' most likely outcome is to see their chapter 11 case dismissed.[108]

And of ultimate importance for this study, the cases in the big dataset involve many more professionals. 59% of the big cases involve at least one retained financial adviser, while less than 12% of the random cases used such professionals. Indeed, more than half of the big cases employed at least three additional professionals, beyond their primary bankruptcy counsel, to help them navigate

106 Lynn LoPucki has recently argued that these "Ordinary Course Professional" motions are "illegal." Lynn M. LoPucki & Joseph W. Doherty, *Routine Illegality in Bankruptcy Court Fee Practices*, 83 Am. Bankr. L.J. 423 (2009). The thesis of the LoPucki article has been roundly contested and criticized in Martin J. Bienenstock et al., *Response to "Routine Illegality in Bankruptcy Court, Big-Case Fee Practices"*, 83 Am. Bankr. L.J. 549 (2009).

107 Contrasted with Warner's classic study of railroad bankruptcies, which found an average length of 13 years, it appears that chapter 11, despite its reputation, is a significant improvement over its predecessors. *See* Jerold B. Warner, *Bankruptcy Costs: Some Evidence*, 32 J. Fin. 337, 340 (1977).

108 *See* Lynn M. LoPucki & William C. Whitford, *Patterns in the Bankruptcy Reorganization of Large, Publicly Held Companies*, 78 Cornell L. Rev. 597, 600-01 (1993) (reporting 96% confirmation rate for bankruptcies of large public companies). A dismissed case leaves the federal bankruptcy system, leaving creditors to their rights under state debtor-creditor law. Typically this involves individual creditor-by-creditor collection of the debts.

chapter 11. Just 11% of the random sample debtors hired that many additional professionals.

Chapter 11 is thus a broad term that hides a wealth of variety. What chapter 11 "is" is largely dependent on the size of the debtor under examination. The big case dataset represents the world addressed by much chapter 11 scholarship and the financial press; the random dataset represents the more typical chapter 11 debtor, a bankrupt firm that is much, much smaller than Lehman Brothers or General Motors

B. Defining Debtor Size

Given the importance of debtor size to any examination of chapter 11, it is remarkable that the question of how to measure size is so infrequently addressed. In many of the early studies of professional fees, the debtor's asset or market value was used without further discussion. Of course, even if one settles on asset size as the measure of size, the next question is which measure of asset size? Assets are often reported several different ways through the course of a chapter 11 case, depending on the particular context and the relevant background legal and accounting rules.

Lynn LoPucki is one of the few scholars to address the issue directly, and he has typically settled on assets listed on the petition as the best measure of debtor size.[109] This measure only works for publicly traded debtors, which are the focus of his studies, as other debtors are not required to complete Exhibit A to the petition.[110] Indeed, many of the routinely utilized measures of size, including equity or debt market values, are not generalizable to the universe of debtor firms that are not required to disclose information and not subject to transparent market pricing.

In a more recent article, Professor LoPucki has turned to the number of debtor employees.[111] The latter measure would seem to treat certain industries as inherently bigger – such as retail and transportation firms – while discounting the size of debtors in areas that are less labor intensive. For example, while Lehman Brothers was amongst the largest recent chapter 11 cases by asset value, measuring size by employees would treat United Airlines as a bigger chapter 11 case.

109 Lynn M. LoPucki and Joseph W. Doherty, *Rise of the Financial Advisors: An Empirical Study of the Division of Professional Fees in Large Bankruptcies*, 82 Am. Bankr. L. J. 141 (2008).

110 Exhibit A to the bankruptcy petition, only required of publicly traded firms, requires information regarding the debtor's publicly traded securities and basic balance sheet information. http://www.uscourts.gov/rules/BK_Forms_1207/B_001A_0997f.pdf.

111 Lynn M. LoPucki & Joseph W. Doherty, *Professional Overcharging in Large Bankruptcy Reorganization Cases*, 5 J. Empirical L. Stud. 983 (2008).

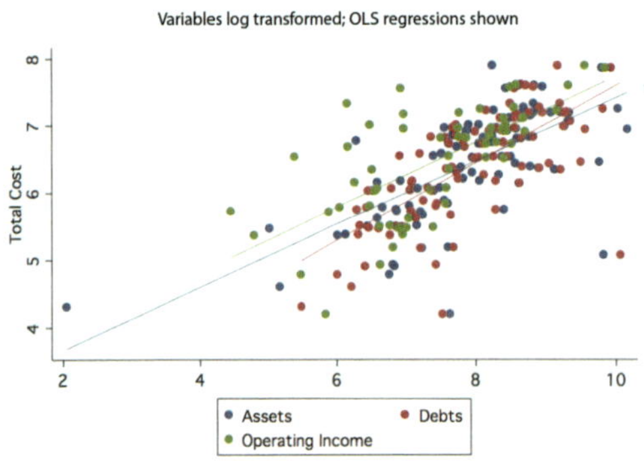

Figure 4: Cost and Size by Various Measures (Big Case Dataset)

In the past I have expressed concern that using assets alone tends to ignore the case where a debtor seeks bankruptcy after a sudden drop in asset values[112] – is this firm better treated according to its new size, or the size when it created its business and capital structure?[113] And a debtor's inability to value its assets upon bankruptcy can lead to understatement of size if the debtor reports a key asset's value as "unknown."

To address these concerns, I have, in the past, used the sum of the debtor's assets and debts to measure size. But doing so ostensibly inflates debtor size, and depresses costs relative to that size, occasionally resulting in confusion. It also makes my figures difficult to compare with prior articles that compare cost to asset value or similar measures of size. Consequently, to increase comprehension and comparability with prior works, in the present study I instead use the average of assets and debts.

Figure 5 shows the simple bivariate relationship between chapter 11 cost and this measure of debtor size, while Figure 4 shows the rough similarity between several obvious measures of debtor size.

112 Stephen J. Lubben, *The Direct Costs of Corporate Reorganization: An Empirical Examination of Professional Fees in Large Chapter 11 Cases*, 74 AM. BANKR. L.J. 509 (2000).

113 Warner, *supra* note 107, at 341, makes a similar point when he argues that firm size should be measured at the point of the financing decision, rather than at bankruptcy, when firm value has undoubtedly already fallen, although Altman rightly notes that the extremely gradual decline in value that Warner found was undoubtedly a product of the specific industry Warner studied. Edward I. Altman, *A Further Empirical Investigation of the Bankruptcy Cost Question*, 39 J. FIN. 1067, 1070 (1984).

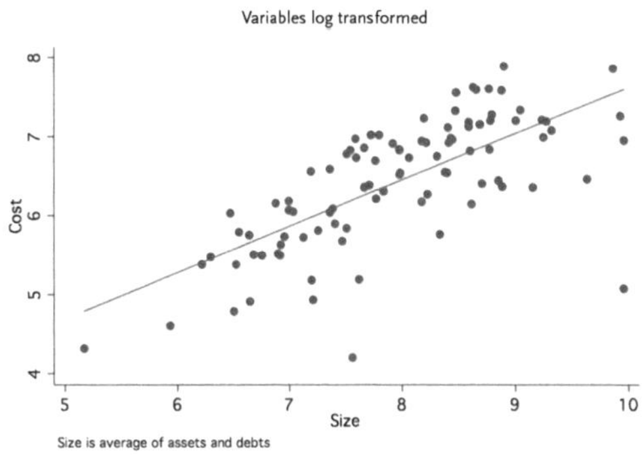

Figure 5: Cost by Size (Big Case Dataset)

Summary

This chapter makes clear the substantial variety in chapter 11 debtors. Under a single process deceptively known as "chapter 11" lurks distinct debtors, and even somewhat distinct processes, given that larger firms are more likely to ask the court to modify chapter 11 to suit their needs and to engage chapter 11 with the help of multiple professionals.

The chapter also introduces the two datasets used in this study. The random dataset includes almost 1,000 "typical" chapter 11 cases, randomly selected from around the United States. The big case dataset includes 97 of the cases that are often of interest – very large debtors, many of which are publicly traded companies.

The cases in the big case dataset are, on average solvent, while the random sample dataset cases are, on average, heavily insolvent. Confirmed plans are much more common among the bigger cases, while the random dataset debtors' most likely outcome is to see their chapter 11 case dismissed.

This chapter also presents a discussion of how debtor size should be measured when examining chapter 11 costs. Ultimately an average of assets and debts is found preferable to either measure standing alone.

Appendix 2B: Variable Descriptions

Assets (000s)	Debtor's total assets
Debts (000s)	Debtor's total debts
Op. In. (000s)	"Operating Income," as reported in Statement of Financing Affairs (SOFA). May not track "operating income" as understood by accountants because of wording of question in SOFA (i.e., might include all income received).
Publicly Traded	Dummy variable; yes indicates debtor files reports with SEC as of petition date
Involuntary	Dummy variable; yes indicates involuntary petition

Appendix 2B (continued)

Prepackaged	Dummy variable; yes indicates prepack case (pre-bankruptcy voting on plan)
DIP Loan	Dummy variable; yes indicates post-bankruptcy financing approved by court
# Lawsuits	Total number of lawsuits pending against debtor, as reported in SOFA
Trustee	Dummy variable; yes indicates trustee appointed
Examiner	Dummy variable; yes indicates examiner appointed
Monthly Comp.	Dummy variable; yes indicates court approved partial payment of professionals on monthly basis (often 80%), pending quarterly fee applications
Ord. C. Prof.	Dummy variable; yes indicates court approved abbreviated procedures for employment and retention of non-bankruptcy professionals billing under set amount.
Claims Agent	Dummy variable; yes indicates court approved use of claims agent to administer claims register
363 Motion	Dummy variable; yes indicates sale of all or substantially all assets before plan
Committee	Dummy variable; yes indicates appointment of at least one committee
Plan Filed	Dummy variable; yes indicates a plan was filed, whether or not confirmed by court
# Classes	Total number of classes in reorganization plan
Sub-debt Class	Dummy variable; yes indicates at least one class of subordinated debt (typically bond debt)
Exit Fin.	Dummy variable; yes indicates plan includes new financing for debtor
Fraud	Dummy variable; yes indicates evidence of fraud or breach of duty by management prebankruptcy
# Claims	Total number of claims filed in debtor's case
First Day	Dummy variable; yes indicates "first day" motions were filed. First day motions request permission to deviate from the Bankruptcy Code or other regulations because compliance would undermine the going concern value of the debtor. For example, a typical motion requests permission to immediately pay employees their priority wage claims, instead of waiting for confirmation of a plan.
# Stay Motions	Total number of motions to lift the automatic stay
# C/D Motions	Total number of motions to convert (to chapter 7) or dismiss the case
# Trustee	Total number of motions to appoint a trustee
Ret. Bonus	Dummy variable; yes indicates a motion to pay retention bonuses to management or employees during the case
3+ Extra Profs.	Dummy variable; yes indicates that the debtor retained three or more professionals beyond bankruptcy counsel
Fin. Adv.	Dummy variable; yes indicates that at least one financial advisor was retained in the case (by debtor or committee)
Days in Ch 11	Total days spent in chapter 11 before conversion, dismissal, or confirmation of a plan

IV The Direct Costs of Chapter 11

In this chapter I develop a general model of professional fees in chapter 11 cases, a model that I then extend to the specific case of attorneys and financial advisers in subsequent chapters. Because most of the existing empirical and theoretical literature deals with very large chapter 11 cases, I first develop the model with respect to the big case dataset and then extend it to the random dataset.

A. Measuring Chapter 11 Cost

In a chapter 11 case, all professionals that are to be paid with estate funds are required to have their retention approved at the start of the case.[114] And the bulk of those professionals[115] are also required to have their fees and expenses approved by the bankruptcy court before being paid from the estate.[116] In short, there is both *ex ante* and *ex post* oversight of most professionals by the bankruptcy court.

The debtor's bankruptcy estate is responsible for paying for all professionals it retained in the case. In addition, the estate is responsible for paying the expenses of any professionals retained by official – that is, court appointed – committees in the case.[117] Finally, the estate is also responsible for paying any court appointed "neutrals," and their professionals, including trustees and examiners. All of these expenses count as costs of administration of the estate, and are thus entitled to priority payment.[118]

The datasets used in this study capture the following fee information of each debtor in the sample:

- The fees and expenses of the debtor's lead bankruptcy counsel
- The fees and expenses of the debtor's local counsel (if any)[119]
- The fees and expenses of up to eight additional debtor professionals, beyond lead and local bankruptcy counsel

---

114 11 U.S.C. §327(a).

115 In larger cases, it has become common to excuse non-bankruptcy "ordinary course" professionals from the formal retention and fee approval system, although this practice is the subject of some controversy. Lynn M. LoPucki & Joseph W. Doherty, *Routine Illegality in Bankruptcy Court Fee Practices*, 83 Am. Bankr. L.J. 423 (2009); *see also* Martin J. Bienenstock et al., *Response to "Routine Illegality in Bankruptcy Court, Big-Case Fee Practices"*, 83 Am. Bankr. L.J. 549 (2009).

116 *See* 11 U.S.C. §§327, 330, 331.

117 11 U.S.C. §§1103; 330

118 11 U.S.C. §§507(a)(2); 503(b)(2).

119 In the United States, attorneys are licensed to practice on a state-by-state basis. Large corporate debtors typically hire "lead" counsel from New York, Chicago, or Los Angeles. But if the debtor's bankruptcy case is filed in a different jurisdiction (*e.g.*, Delaware) the debtor will also have to hire "local" counsel admitted to the bar of that state, unless the firm in question has a local office in the state in question.

And the study also collects the following information for up to three official committees in each case:

- The fees and expenses of the committee's lead bankruptcy counsel
- The fees and expenses of the committee's local bankruptcy counsel (if any)
- The fees and expenses of up to two additional professionals for each committee, beyond lead and local bankruptcy counsel

The number limitations on the "extra professional" fields are a result of the Excel data entry form, which was designed in consultation with various bankruptcy professionals. Although before the study it was widely felt that eight additional professional debtor fields were sufficient, in seventeen cases all eight fields were utilized, and it can be supposed that in some of these cases there were more than eight additional debtor professionals retained. The majority of cost will be captured in these cases, as the principal professionals will be captured, but there undoubtedly will be some censoring of cost.

The datasets also include information on the costs of trustees, examiners, and fee examiners, along with the costs of professionals retained by these parties.[120] And the study also captures the pre-bankruptcy professional fees and expenses paid by the debtors and reported on their statement of financial affairs.

The sum of all these fees and expenses form the measure of chapter 11 costs used throughout this study.

In the big case dataset, the average case incurred over $8.4 million ($3.7 million median) in total professional costs.[121] Alternatively stated, the debtors in this dataset incurred almost $34,000 ($11,795) per day in chapter 11 – although costs are not incurred in a uniform manner, indeed the cost of a chapter 11 case seems to ebb and flow with certain key events (petition filing, plan confirmation), in many cases it is heavily front-loaded. This latter effect may reflect the extra work involved in stabilizing the debtor's business after a chapter 11 filing.

Frequent references to a professional's "burn rate" are thus misleading, inasmuch as it implies a fixed or constant cost to chapter 11. The "lumpiness" of chapter 11 costs can be seen in Figure 6, which shows the month-by-month charges of lead bankruptcy counsel in a single Delaware chapter 11 case.[122]

120 This does not include fees and expenses of claims agents or professionals retained under an "ordinary course professional" motion. Claims agents are typically paid in the "ordinary course" and thus do not file fee applications with the court.

121 Big case dataset:

	Mean	Std. Err.	[95% Conf.	Interval]
Total cost	$8,408,187.00	$1,380,296.00	$5,667,953.00	$11,100,000.00
Cost per day	$33,708.62	$5,710.50	$22,371.84	$45,045.40
n=96				

122 Note that the first fee application includes two months.

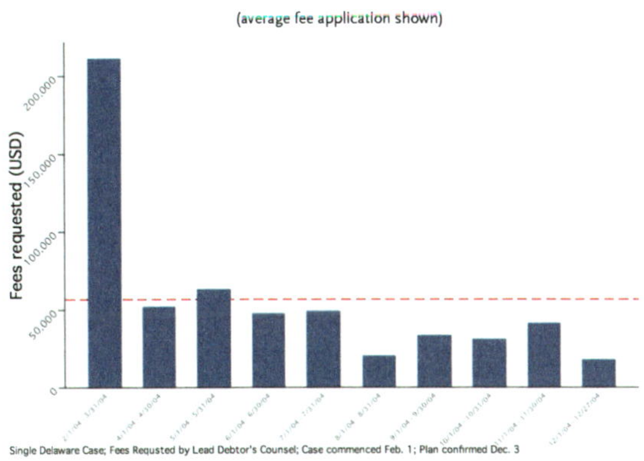

Figure 6: Fees Requested in Each Fee Application (Big Case Dataset)

Debtor professionals were, on average, responsible for 63.1% (64.7% median) of total cost.[123] Committee costs were 40.2% (32.3%) of debtor costs, or 22.5% (21.9%) of total chapter 11 costs.

Throughout the literature, it has become common to report fees as a percentage of debtor size. The advantage of such a measure is obvious – namely it provides an easy "rule of thumb" for considering whether a particular case is above or below the average cost. But as Professor LoPucki has noted, the relationship between debtor size and cost is highly sensitive to the size of the cases under study, meaning that use of such "rules of thumb" will often result in substantial errors.

123 Big case dataset:

	Mean	Std. Err.	[95% Conf.	Interval]
Comm. over Debtor (n=72)	0.402	0.032	0.338	0.466
Comm. over Total (n=72)	0.225	0.011	0.203	0.247
Debtor over Total (n=93)	0.631	0.021	0.589	0.672

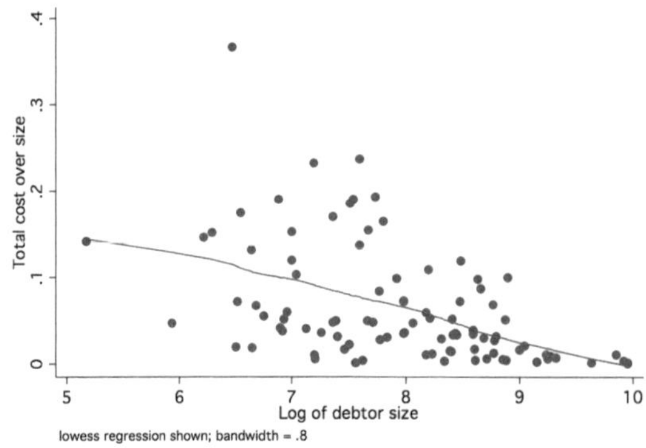

Figure 7A: Cost/Size Ratio by Debtor Size (Big Case Dataset)

This same effect is evident in the present study, where the average cost of the smallest quartile of cases is 10% of size,[124] while in the largest cases cost is 2% of size. Based on the ratios of cost to size shown on Table 7B, it appears that there are substantial economies of scale to chapter 11 cases, a relationship that is also examined in Figure 7A.[125] The relationship between size and standardized cost demonstrates a strong downward trend, further suggesting that there may be significant fixed costs to chapter 11, and thus a declining cost for the largest of debtors.

Table 7B: Standardized Chapter 11 Cost by Size Quartiles (Big Case Dataset)

	Mean	*Std. Err.*	*[95% Conf.*	*Interval]*
Total cost over size				
1 (smallest)	0.101	0.017	0.067	0.135
2	0.089	0.015	0.059	0.119
3	0.042	0.006	0.029	0.055
4	0.021	0.006	0.010	0.033
Mean debtor size (USD)				
1	7,080,907.00	981,618.40	5,131,608.00	9,030,207.00
2	44,700,000.00	4,120,754.00	36,500,000.00	52,900,000.00
3	242,000,000.00	21,800,000.00	198,000,000.00	285,000,000.00
4	2,410,000,000.00	609,000,000.00	1,200,000,000.00	3,620,000,000.00

n=94

124 Defined as the average of assets and debts, see Chapter 3.

125 The outlier at the top of the graph represents the chapter 11 case of Mid-State Raceway, Inc., the owner of a horse-racing track and affiliated hotel in northern New York State. In re Mid-State Raceway, Inc., 04-65746, 2006 BL 27793 (Bankr. N.D.N.Y. Feb. 10, 2006) (opinion confirming chapter 11 plan). It is unclear from reviewing the case file why the case appears so relatively expensive, although gambling is heavily regulated in the United States and it may be that this extra regulation resulted in additional cost.

B. Determinants of Cost

Figure 8 begins the consideration of this topic by plotting the various factors that might influence the overall cost of chapter 11 on a graph that shows the bivariate relationship between cost and debtor size. A review of the graph suggests that cases with committees and 363 sales might be cheaper, while New York and Delaware cases might be more expensive. But because the relationships might be complex, it is hard to draw definitive conclusions from a simple review of bivariate relationships.

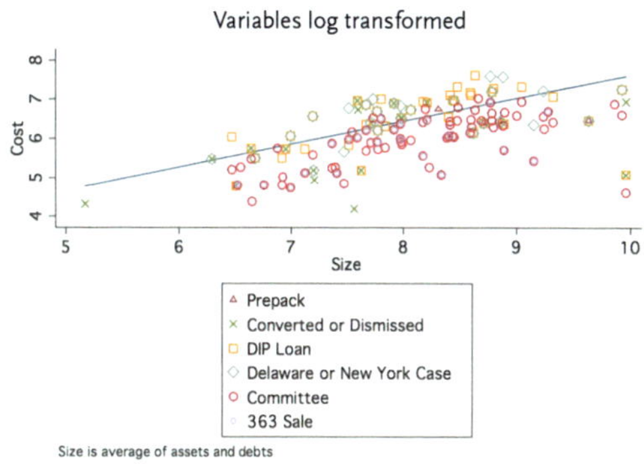

Figure 8: Factors in Cost (Big Case Dataset)

Figure 8 also shows that the bivariate relationship between size and cost is not linear – flattening out somewhat on the right side among the biggest cases. Almost every case larger than $ 1 billion (log 9) falls below the regression line, suggesting costs are lower than would be predicted by a direct linear relationship. As I show in the final models below, there is an element of complexity in these cases that is not captured by size alone. An oversimplified model ignores this non-linearity and puts too much stress on the size variable. By modeling complexity distinct from size, the models shown on Table 10 address this aspect of cost.

* * *

Debtor size is the most obvious determinant of the cost of chapter 11. All else equal, a larger firm will be more expensive to reorganize because it has more contracts, employees, assets and other issues to deal with in its bankruptcy case, and professionals typically charge clients based on either the actual or estimated amount of time a particular task will demand.

This might also suggest that the length of a chapter 11 case should determine its cost, although to some degree this conflates the total number of professional hours a particular case requires with the duration of the case. At least in larger chapter 11 cases, the total number of hours expended on a particular case is a function of how many hours a particular professional expends on that case, the hourly rates charged, *and* the number of professionals working on the matter. Only the first factor is evidently effected by the case duration.[126]

Thus I would hypothesize that debtor size should have a positive effect on cost, and, time should have little or no effect on cost. But we should also consider that size, like time, is a kind of "catch all" factor that probably acts as a proxy for factors that can be more clearly modeled. Thus, we should expect size to decrease in overall importance in more elaborate models.

Several prior studies have found that prepackaged chapter 11 cases incurred lower professional fees, although these studies typically do not consider professional fees incurred before the bankruptcy petition is filed with the court. As noted in Lubben (2000), the design of these studies may capture nothing more than time shifting of professional fees in prepackaged cases. And while this study captures pre-bankruptcy professional fees reported on the statement of financial affairs, that statement is often not filed in prepackaged cases, meaning that this study would suffer from a similar difficulty.

But under the Bankruptcy Code,[127] attorneys are required to disclose compensation they received before the petition was filed, and as part of the additional data collection done for this study, I gathered this information for the attorneys' retention applications in prepackaged cases.[128] Thus I hypothesize that filing a prepackaged case will have no effect on overall cost, but rather results in the shifting of costs, such as the cost of drafting a plan, to the pre-bankruptcy period.[129]

Other similar factors that might reduce cost include 363 sales, which should somewhat reduce the difficulty of plan negotiations by converting the debtor's assets into cash, and conversion or dismissal of the chapter 11 case.[130] The last two factors would bring the debtor's chapter 11 expenses to a quick end, albeit with uncertain effects on the debtor's total costs of financial distress, depending on the relative costs of state law collection and chapter 7 liquidation, but that is beyond the scope of the present study.

Additionally, the complexity of the chapter 11 case, distinct from the debtor's size, might influence cost. One indicator of complexity is the debtor's retention of additional professionals beyond bankruptcy counsel. In this paper I use the

126 In the ABI Chapter 11 Fee Study, I found no relationship between time and total cost. But that study only covered large chapter 11 cases for two years, so there might have been a relationship that was hidden by the study design. Accordingly, I will re-examine case duration in the present model.

127 11 U.S.C. §329(a).

128 This approach will still underestimate the total cost of prepackaged cases, inasmuch as it does not capture the costs of any "ad hoc" bondholder committees or financial advisers paid by the debtor before the case was commenced.

129 As it turns out, the conventional wisdom is not supported by this dataset even without inclusion of the pre-petition fees. Rather, as discussed in connection with Table 10.1, *infra*, prepackaged cases only appear "cheaper" if the prepetition fees are omitted *and* intra-jurisdictional correlations are ignored.

130 Harvey R. Miller, *Chapter 11 in Transition – From Boom to Bust and Into the Future*, 81 AM. BANKR. L.J. 375, 385 (2007).

debtor's retention of more than three additional professionals as an indicator of a particularly complex case. This complexity might come from the debtor's financial structure, or it might simply come from the scale of the debtor's business. For example, even a purely domestic debtor often needs to retain counsel familiar with the laws of the individual states in which it operates.

In addition, one might surmise that there is a group of extremely complex cases that is even more complex than the typical large chapter 11 case – that is, cases like United Airlines or Lehman Brothers might be different from a merely large chapter 11 case.[131]

In this study I utilize several dummy variables to capture these extremely complex cases. First, I use a variable that asks if the debtor implemented an "ordinary course professionals" (OCP) process in the case. As previously discussed, these motions essentially ask for an exception to the usual rule that all debtor professionals must file formal retention and fee applications before they can be retained or paid. Instead, the debtor asks the court to approve abbreviated procedures for professionals who are largely exogenous to the chapter 11 process.[132]

It may seem that OCP motions should reduce the reported cost of a case, since an OCP system removes professionals from the total cost used as the dependent variable. But the total cost of these professionals is small, averaging less than $100,000 per month.[133] In short, it is arguable that the presence or absence of an OPC motion will be of little import to the dependent variable.

I also consider the interaction of this variable with the prior variable that asks if the debtor retained three or more professionals, beyond bankruptcy counsel. The interaction term captures those cases where the debtor both implemented an OCP system and hired three or more professionals. The interaction variable should capture those cases where the debtor has highly "professionalized" its chapter 11 case – if we assume that the non-bankruptcy professionals are largely removed from the dependent variable by means of the OCP system. This variable should also capture the non-linearity seen amongst the largest cases back on Figure 8.

I also include a dummy variable that indicates whether or not a committee was appointed in the case. Obviously the appointment of a committee almost directly leads to the retention of additional professionals, especially in larger cases.[134]

131 There are two ways of looking at this aspect of extremely large chapter 11 cases: either one can consider it additional complexity, as I do in this study, or one could consider it an aspect of size that is not captured by simple balance-sheet measures of size. There is no obvious way of distinguishing between these two interpretations of the effects modeled herein.

132 As might be expected, this variable is correlated with debtor size (0.439; $p<0.05$). But once size is separately accounted for in the following models, the presence of an OCP motion can be interpreted as a complexity measure.

133 For the 32 cases with available data on this point. The median is just over $32,000 per month. The cost of filing full retention and compensation applications, if the professionals were not subject to the abbreviated procedures, might well equal or exceed the cost of their non-bankruptcy work, which raises the issue of whether OCP motions might not reduce the cost of chapter 11 cases.

134 In some smaller cases, committees do not retain professionals.

Beyond simply capturing the number of professionals in a case, however, both the committee and additional debtor professionals variables can also be seen as indicators of case complexity, especially if we presume that the bankruptcy court exercises at least a minimal degree of oversight over the debtor's retention of additional professionals and the appointment of committees. The appointment of a committee also increases the number of key parties in the case that debtor's counsel must consult, potentially increasing overall costs in a way that is not captured by simply counting the total number of professionals retained in a case.

I also consider if a claims agent has been appointed in the case. As my dependent variable does not include the cost of the claims agent, in this context the claims agent acts as a pure proxy for a complex chapter 11 process, where the debtor anticipates the need for extra "help" reconciling the claims register.

In addition, Professor LoPucki has been extremely critical of the tendency to file large chapter 11 cases in New York and Delaware, jurisdictions that he views as the source of a larger pattern of judicial "corruption." As part of this criticism, he has suggested that these jurisdictions are associated with higher professional fees, as he asserts that the judges do not wish to drive large corporate bankruptcy cases to other courts.[135] Accordingly, I use dummy variables to indicate whether or not a case was filed in New York or Delaware. Under the thesis implied by Professor LoPucki's criticism, these variables should be positively related to cost.[136]

Moreover, the financial press has recently focused on the high hourly rates charged by some "big city" law firms in chapter 11 cases.[137] Under the implicit thesis of these articles – namely, that high rates translate into higher chapter 11 costs – these high hourly rates should correlate with higher chapter 11 costs. On the other hand, in prior work I have noted that most of the cost of a chapter 11 case comes from the middle of the rate structure.[138] I input the highest hourly rate charged by debtor's counsel to examine both issues; the highest rate not only implicates the popular fascination with the top rate, but also addresses the mid-tier attorneys in that their hourly rates are likely to be highly correlated with the top rates, and high top rates are apt to indicate higher middle rates.

Finally, it should be expected that the presence of court appointed neutrals in a case will increase the cost, particularly when those neutrals are additional costs in the reorganization process. Thus I consider all three types of neutrals – trustees, examiners, and fee examiners – that are coded in the datasets. Examiners,

135 In the United States, a large corporate debtor typically has a choice of where to file their bankruptcy case, because the case can be filed in any jurisdiction where any individual member of the corporate group might file a case (typically either where its headquarters are or its state of incorporation).

136 Of course, LoPucki has also argued that the objectionable procedures in these jurisdictions have spread to other districts, which may make his thesis untestable. It should also imply that there is no longer any benefit from filing in New York or Delaware, yet debtors continue to seek out these jurisdictions (*e.g.*, GM and Chrysler).

137 http://www.nytimes.com/2010/05/02/business/02workout.html?hp.

138 Stephen J. Lubben, *The Microeconomics of Chapter 11*, Part 2, 4 INT'L. CORP. RESCUE 87 (2007); *The Microeconomics of Chapter 11*, Part 1, 4 INT'L. CORP. RESCUE 31 (2007).

appointed to investigate and report on the debtor's or some creditor's conduct, should add to the costs of a case both directly and by indicating a case with a particular degree of tension between the debtor and its creditors.[139] The effects of appointment of a trustee should be similar, although the effect might be mitigated by the fact that the trustee typically usurps the debtor and its professionals, meaning that a trustee might have a neutral effect on overall cost.

Fee examiners present a more complex state of affairs. Conventional wisdom suggests that fee examiners should reduce cost, after all the primary purpose of a fee examiner is to provide a kind of "audit" of professional fees in a chapter case.[140] But in previous work I found that the fee examiners actually seemed to increase cost, although the effect was not statistically significant.[141]

This is consistent with the suspicion that the cost of fee examiners exceeds their benefit, as least with regard to actual fee reduction. To be sure, fee examiners provide some administrative benefits to the bankruptcy court, which might be otherwise overwhelmed by the number of fee applications in a large chapter 11 case, but those benefits, and whether fee examiners are the proper solution to this problem, are hard to gauge. Thus I hypothesize that, contrary to conventional wisdom, the appointment of a fee examiner should increase overall cost in the chapter 11 process.

* * *

Before addressing the model, I should note that I do not use three variables that many readers might consider especially relevant: the ratio of secured debt to total debt, the overall leverage of the debtor and the number of classes in the debtor's plan. The solvency or leverage of the debtor intuitively seems to be related to chapter 11 cost, but that relationship is actually quite complex upon further examination.

For example, it may be that a debtor on the margin of solvency will incur more chapter 11 cost because the shareholders will have stronger incentives to argue about the valuation of the debtor. On the other hand, at some point of insolvency, further insolvency does not matter, provided it comes in the form of unsecured debt, in that the debtor likely does not care if its $100 million or $500 million of bond debt that gets discharged.

The ratio of secured debt to overall debt might be important for cost, in that secured creditors have a more robust set of legal rights and powers under American law. But data on secured debt is often missing in the big case sample, driving the total number of cases down into the low 70s. I do use this variable in the random dataset, *infra*, where the size of the dataset overcomes the problem of missing data.

139 See Jonathan C. Lipson, *Understanding Failure: Examiners And The Bankruptcy Reorganization Of Large Public Companies*, 84 AM BANKR. L.J. 1 (2010).
140 http://amlawdaily.typepad.com/amlawdaily/2010/01/feesthornburg.html.
141 Lubben (2008).

Despite the foregoing, I did test both variables as final additions to the models presented here. The ratio of secured debt to overall debt was not significant in the model, albeit with a smaller sample size. And while the debtor's asset to debt ratio was significant, it added little to the overall model, increasing the R-squared by 0.02, while providing a host of interpretive problems outlined above.

Finally, I did not use the number of classes in the debtor's plan as a proxy for complexity of capital structure, because the number of classes can also reflect the plan proponent's manipulation of the chapter 11 voting rules. Moreover, the capital structure of the multiple corporate entities that make up a single enterprise can often be classified in myriad ways, making the variable more reflective of the attorney that drafted or negotiated the plan than anything else.

* * *

Table 8.1, on the next page, examines the relationship among the variables used in the models. As shown, several of the "complexity" variables are correlated with debtor size. This provides an independent reason to control for debtor size, even if that variable itself is not significant, so that the complexity measures can capture complexity itself, without also measuring size.

Table 8.1: Pairwise Correlations of Variables in Models on Table 10

	Log of debtor size	*Case converted to ch. 7*	*Case dismissed*	*Pre-packaged case*	*363 motion*	*Log of days in ch. 11*	*3+ professionals*	*OCP system*	*Interaction OCP & 3+*	*Official committee*	*Claims agent*	*Case from SDNY*	*Delaware case*	*Highest hourly rate*	*Trustee*	*Examiner*	*Fee examiner*
Log of debtor size	1																
Case converted to ch. 7	-0.1183	1															
Case dismissed	-0.0967	-0.1144	1														
Prepackaged case	0.2052*	-0.0663	-0.0742	1													
363 motion	-0.1043	0.1274	0.0038	-0.1255	1												
Log of days in ch. 11	-0.1419	-0.0472	0.1035	-0.5530*	0.2725*	1											
3+ professionals	0.3066*	-0.1001	-0.2372*	-0.0414	0.0215	0.2416*	1										
OCP system	0.4387*	-0.0448	-0.2933*	0.0414	-0.0215	-0.0412	0.2436*	1									
Interaction OCP & 3+	0.4158*	-0.0536	-0.2336*	-0.0222	-0.0393	0.1294	0.5355*	0.7964*	1								
Official committee	0.2912*	0.0035	-0.2721*	-0.3829*	0.0161	0.4248*	0.2588*	0.2935*	0.2999*	1							
Claims agent	0.5523*	-0.0902	-0.2745*	0.1145	-0.1086	-0.1268	0.3156*	0.4002*	0.3719*	0.2679*	1						
Case from SDNY	0.0068	-0.0302	0.0382	0.2099*	-0.1161	-0.1266	-0.0222	0.082	0.0522	-0.1979	0.2562*	1					
Delaware case	0.1403	-0.0215	-0.0453	0.0706	0.1035	-0.0672	0.0757	-0.014	-0.0586	0.0685	0.2324*	-0.1616	1				
Highest hourly rate	0.6043*	-0.0591	-0.205	0.220*	-0.0695	-0.1126	0.2170*	0.4493*	0.3228*	0.1597	0.6873*	0.2476*	0.2093*	1			
Trustee	-0.155	0.2916*	0.011	-0.0622	-0.0968	0.1793	-0.1363	-0.093	-0.0321	0.0729	-0.0596	0.0902	-0.1179	-0.014	1		
Examiner	0.0526	0.0654	-0.0918	-0.0533	0.0379	0.1413	0.1233	0.0513	0.1128	0.0369	0.0133	-0.1055	-0.101	0.019	-0.077	1	
Fee examiner	0.1991	0.0654	-0.0918	-0.0533	0.1345	0.1028	0.2106	0.1386	0.2062*	0.1391	0.2704*	0.0163	0.2758*	0.2264*	-0.077	-0.0659	1

* $p < 0.05$

1

C. The Model

To model the total cost of these large chapter 11 cases, I enter the foregoing variables in a series of blocks, grouping the variables by concept, as follows:

Model 1: Debtor size

Model 2: Debtor size, time-related variables

Model 3: Debtor size, time-related variables, complexity variables

Model 4: Debtor size, time-related variables, complexity variables, mega case variables

Model 5: Debtor size, time-related variables, complexity variables, mega case variables, court-appointed neutrals

Entering the variables in this manner facilitates understanding of the work done by each group of explanatory factors in the larger model. The five models are set forth on Table 10, with descriptive statistics for the 87 cases used in the model set forth on Appendix 10A at the end of this section.

Because of extreme skewness and non-normal distributions, the three continuous variables – cost, size, and time – are transformed with a log base-10 transformation.[142] Figure 9 shows the results of the transformations.

Finally, throughout this study I account for the grouping of cases by judicial district and the potential correlation of cases on that basis by adjusting the standard errors to control for this effect.[143] While Stata automatically invokes robust standard errors in connection with clustered standard errors, pre-testing of the regressions indicated heteroskedasticity, so robust standard errors would have been called for in any event.[144]

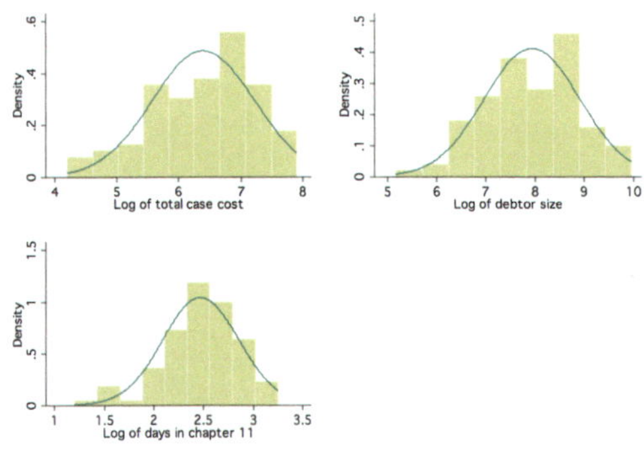

Figure 9: Transformed Variables

142 This same transformation can be seen in several of the Figures in Chapter 3.

143 In particular, I use the "cluster" option in Stata to produce standard errors that account for within judicial district correlations. *See generally* David M. Primo et al., *Estimating the Impact of State Policies and Institutions with Mixed-Level Data*, 7 State and Policy Q. 446 (2007).

144 As shown, *infra*, Appendix 10C, these measures appear to have addressed the heteroskedasticity.

Table 10: Models of Chapter 11 Costs (Big Case Dataset)

	(1)	(2)	(3)	(4)	(5)
	Log of total case cost	*Log of total case cost*	*Log of total case cost*	*Log of total case cost*	*Log of total case cost*
Log of debtor size	0.573***	0.575***	0.277*	0.213	0.232
	(0.0866)	(0.0874)	(0.112)	(0.120)	(0.122)
Case converted to ch. 7		-0.447	-0.341	-0.340	-0.454*
		(0.309)	(0.224)	(0.194)	(0.198)
Case dismissed		-0.607	0.0169	0.0338	0.0495
		(0.323)	(0.213)	(0.202)	(0.216)
Prepackaged Case		-0.114	0.0774	0.0318	-0.0289
		(0.257)	(0.296)	(0.345)	(0.340)
363 Motion		0.0224	0.0342	0.0463	0.0424
		(0.130)	(0.105)	(0.0999)	(0.0995)
Log of days in chapter 11		0.429	0.185	0.140	0.0948
		(0.211)	(0.182)	(0.163)	(0.189)
3+ professionals			0.591***	0.590***	0.629***
			(0.160)	(0.141)	(0.140)
OCP system			0.672***	0.545***	0.628***
			(0.160)	(0.147)	(0.149)
Interaction, OCP & 3+			-0.367*	-0.320*	-0.401*
			(0.159)	(0.156)	(0.169)
Official committee			0.250	0.290	0.237
			(0.181)	(0.164)	(0.174)
Claims agent			0.413**	0.274	0.293*
			(0.132)	(0.138)	(0.129)
Case from SDNY				-0.0960	-0.0855
				(0.0748)	(0.0764)
Delaware case				-0.212**	-0.179*
				(0.0715)	(0.0853)
Highest hourly rate				0.00110*	0.000923*
				(0.000469)	(0.000428)
Trustee					0.230
					(0.158)
Examiner					0.635**
					(0.194)
Fee examiner					0.0469
					(0.193)
Constant	1.876**	0.898	2.861**	2.979***	3.003**
	(0.656)	(1.064)	(0.886)	(0.788)	(0.859)
Observations	87	87	87	87	87
$R2$	0.478	0.586**	0.800***	0.830***	0.851*
Adjusted $R2$	0.471	0.555	0.771	0.797	0.815

Robust standard errors in parentheses; se adjusted for clustering by judicial district; mean VIF (Model 5) 2.06

* $p < 0.05$, ** $p < 0.01$, *** $p < 0.001$

The first model considers the simple bivariate relationship between cost and size, a relationship that has already been shown graphically in several of the prior figures. As shown, just under half of the total variance in chapter 11 cost can be explained by the debtor's size alone.[145]

Model 2, which introduces the time-related variables into the model, explains an additional 10% of the variance in chapter 11 costs. Conversion of the case to chapter 7, case dismissal and time spent in chapter 11 are not significant in explaining the cost of chapter 11. Conversion of the case will be significant by Model 5, however.

Throughout all of the models, prepackaged cases do not appear to be any cheaper than traditional chapter 11 cases, once we account for at least some of the pre-bankruptcy costs of these cases. This is consistent with the hypothesis that prepackaged cases shift costs into the pre-bankruptcy period, but do not otherwise significantly reduce the costs of reorganization. Prepackaged cases are only "cheaper" chapter 11 cases in the sense that the fees recorded after the petition is filed are lower.[146] Table 10.1, set forth on the next page, shows the final model from Table 10, this time run without inclusion of pre-petition attorneys fees for the prepackaged cases. The prepackaged variable is still not significant.

Model 3 on Table 10 then introduces the case complexity variables to the model, and all of the variables are initially significant. Importantly, the interaction term – which captures cases that had both ordinary course professional systems and where the debtor retained three or more professionals, beyond bankruptcy counsel – has a negative coefficient throughout the models. This suggests that subdividing bankruptcy work amongst several professionals is not itself a factor in increasing chapter 11 cost.

More importantly, and contrary to popular intuition, this coefficient demonstrates that at some point additional complexity is actually associated with reduced cost. To be sure, the overall effect of having both three or more professionals and an OCP system is positive, as the sum of all three coefficients is positive. But the negative sign on the interaction coefficient results in lower total cost than the simple sum of the two other variables.

This comports with the effect seen in Figure 8, where the largest cases, on the extreme right side of the graph, are below the cost that would be predicted by a simple linear relationship. This points to economies of scale with regard to the largest cases, particularly those over $1 billion in size.

145 Since version 5, when the clustering commands were updated, Stata has not provided adjusted R-squares with clustered standard errors. On Table 10 I have hand calculated adjusted R-squares for those readers would like to see them.

146 Conceivably prepackaged cases might also result in lower *indirect* costs of reorganization too.

Table 10.1: Model of Chapter 11 Costs, Without Pre-bankruptcy Attorney Costs

	(1) *Log of total case cost – no prepack pre-bankruptcy attny fees*
Log of debtor size	0.234
	(0.122)
Case converted to ch. 7	-0.457*
	(0.198)
Case dismissed	0.0553
	(0.216)
Prepackaged case	-0.572
	(0.377)
363 motion	0.0415
	(0.100)
Log of days in ch. 11	0.0911
	(0.191)
3+ professionals	0.643***
	(0.141)
OCP system	0.659***
	(0.155)
Interaction, OCP & 3+	-0.428*
	(0.176)
Official committee	0.231
	(0.175)
Claims agent	0.293*
	(0.131)
Case from SDNY	-0.0989
	(0.0816)
Delaware case	-0.176
	(0.0872)
Highest hourly rate	0.000879*
	(0.000429)
Trustee	0.242
	(0.159)
Examiner	0.642**
	(0.195)
Fee examiner	0.0524
	(0.194)
Constant	3.013**
	(0.864)
Observations	87
$R2$	0.852

Robust standard errors in parentheses; se adjusted for clustering by district

* $p < 0.05$, ** $p < 0.01$, *** $p < 0.001$

Three other indicators of case complexity are also significant in this model, and in the final model. Retention of three or more additional professionals, appointment of a claims agent, and use of an OCP system are all indicative of higher chapter 11 costs. It should be noted that because of inclusion of the interaction variable, when considered alone the OCP and three or more professional variables should be interpreted as indicating those cases where only one of these factors is present.

This model now explains 80% of the total chapter 11 costs. Model 3 thus presents a fairly simple model that explains the bulk of chapter 11 costs, using readily available data.[147]

Model 4 represents an incremental improvement over Model 3, but its results are extremely important, in that many defy conventional expectations. First, cases filed in the Southern District of New York or Delaware are not more expensive than cases filed in other jurisdictions. Indeed, while only the Delaware variable is independently significant, their negative signs suggest that cases filed in these jurisdictions are actually less expensive than cases in other jurisdictions. This might reflect the benefit that comes from the familiarity these courts have with large chapter 11 cases.

Moreover, the highest hourly rate charged by the debtor's lead counsel is also significant. Based on my prior work, I interpret this as an indication that, holding all else equal, a higher hourly rate structure results in higher cost. On one level this is self-evident, but it might also indicate an additional element of complexity that was missed by my prior variables, if the more expensive bankruptcy counsel is hired in more complicated cases. Even if this is true, one would have to worry that the effect might be at least partially confounded by the agency problems inherent in large corporations, which give managers incentives to retain better professionals than the debtor might actually need.

To further examine the complex relationship between size, complexity, and jurisdiction, I considered several additional variations on the final model shown on Table 10. First, I removed the complexity related variables (i.e., all variables added in Model 3 on Table 10). The sign on both jurisdictional variables remained negative, although the jurisdictional variables were no longer significant and the size variable became significant ($p=0.006$). The R-squared for this model was 0.708. This suggests that complexity is hidden in size, and probably confounds the jurisdictional issues too, as so many large cases are in Delaware and New York. Only when complexity is unpacked from size do we see the distinct jurisdictional effects.

But removing the complexity variables not only puts extra stress on size, it also increases the likelihood that the highest hourly rate variable will begin to do the work of the now removed complexity variables. Indeed, the high hourly rate coefficient gets substantially larger in this altered model.

147 The question of why the larger debtors need the additional professionals, and whether these professionals are part of the bankruptcy process or exogenous non-bankruptcy actors, is something that is not easily answered with the present dataset.

Removing this variable from the model has several predictable effects. First, the coefficient on the size variable increased. Second, the R-squared dropped by approximately 0.10. And finally, the sign on the jurisdictional variables switched, as these variables themselves start to pick up a confused mix of jurisdictional and complexity factors that are not captured by any other variables in the altered model.

As a final investigation of this important issue, I returned the complexity variables to the model, but removed the jurisdictional variables. The R-squared for this model was 84.7. All of the same variables that are significant in Model 5 on Table 10 remained significant in this revised model.

* * *

In Model 5, I then consider the effect of court-appointed neutrals. Only the appointment of an examiner is significant. This result itself is unsurprising, as the appointment of an examiner, who conducts an investigation at the expense of the bankruptcy estate, not only reflects the direct expense of the investigation but also the conflict that resulted in that investigation.

However, the results for fee examiners again challenge the conventional wisdom of the financial press and the bankruptcy community. Appointment of a fee examiner does not significantly influence chapter 11 costs. They provide administrative assistance to courts, perhaps reducing the burden represented by fee applications, but fee examiners do not reduce costs. Indeed, the positive sign on this coefficient is suggestive of the opposite relationship.

Debtor size remains a significant determinate of cost throughout the early models, although as predicted its importance in the model declines as further factors are introduced. By the final model, size is not significant (p=0.066).[148] I suggest that prior papers that relied on size were in fact modeling a bundle of size-related concepts, like complexity of the chapter 11 case.

This should not be taken to mean that size has no relationship to cost. Rather, size included alone captures something more than size quo size.[149] Only by unpacking the various size related concepts, and separately modeling the same, can the determinates of chapter 11 cost be fully understood.

148 Throughout I use p=0.05 as my standard of statistical significance.

149 As shown on Appendix 10B, *infra*, the effect is not the result of colliniearity between size and the newly introduced variables, despite the bivariate correlation between the variables shown on Table 8.1.

Table 10.2: Revised Models of Chapter 11 Costs (Big Case Dataset)

	(1) Log of total case cost	(2) Log of total case cost
Case converted to chapter 7	-0.441***	-0.423**
	(0.119)	(0.132)
3+ professionals	0.709***	0.663***
	(0.154)	(0.140)
OCP system	0.662***	0.621***
	(0.169)	(0.128)
Interaction, OCP & 3+	-0.301	-0.342*
	(0.218)	(0.154)
Claims agent	0.372**	0.299*
	(0.109)	(0.111)
Delaware case	-0.134*	-0.157**
	(0.0586)	(0.0488)
Highest hourly rate	0.00130***	0.000770
	(0.000290)	(0.000401)
Examiner	0.663**	0.701**
	(0.191)	(0.199)
Log of debtor size		0.249*
		(0.109)
Constant	4.938***	3.349***
	(0.175)	(0.652)
Observations	87	87
R2	0.765	0.817*

Robust standard errors in parentheses; se adjusted for clustering by district; mean VIF (model 2) 2.11
** p < 0.05, ** p < 0.01, *** p < 0.001*

The limited independent effect of debtor size can be seen on Table 10.2. The first model includes all variables that were significant (p<0.05) from model 5 on Table 9. With just this handful of variables – *not* including debtor size – we can explain more than 75% of the variance in chapter 11 costs. Model 2 adds debtor size. The increase in r-squared is significant (p=0.0293) and explains an additional five percent of the variance in cost.

Interestingly, only in Model 2 does the interaction term, of three or more professionals with an OCP motion, become significant, which may suggest a previously unexplained joint effect, perhaps reflecting an element of complexity that the interaction term does not capture alone. The highest hourly rate variable also becomes insignificant in the second model, which may support the earlier suggestion that higher hourly rates are associated with larger, more complex debtors.

Finally, note that in all models time spent in chapter 11 is not a significant determinate of cost in any of the models on Table 10.[150] The conventional wisdom that long, drawn out chapter 11 cases are directly linked to higher chapter 11 costs ignores the ways in which modern American corporate law firms are unlike the solicitors in *Bleak House*.[151] While the latter clearly benefited from extending the length of a case, the former would achieve the same end by either extending the case or heavily staffing the case.[152] That is, chapter 11 costs are a bit like an American football or British rugby ball, whose overall volume does not change even if its width varies depending on which side is measured.

Figure 10.3 shows the overall performance of the final model – in a model that perfectly predicted cost, all of the individual cases (represented as circles) would line up on the regression line, or within the confidence intervals that are also shown on Figure 10.3. In sum, the graph suggests that Model 5 performs reasonably well, with no obvious group of deviant cases.

Figure 10.3: Predicted vs. Observed Chapter 11 Costs (Final Model)

150 Time spent in chapter 11 does not influence the professional fees associated with the case. Of course, the creditors experience losses related to the time value of money if the case takes longer to pay out recoveries.

151 CHARLES DICKENS, BLEAK HOUSE (1853).

152 Of course, all of this turns on a degree of cynicism about lawyers that I do not share, and supposes that the debtor's management and creditors have no ability to prevent evident manipulation of a case's length or overstaffing.

Appendix 10A: Descriptive Statistics for Models on Table 10 (Big Case Dataset)

Number of obs. = 87	*Mean*	*Std. Dev.*	*Min*	*Max*
Dependent (Log of total costs)	6.418	0.805	4.200	7.891
Log of debtor size	7.931	0.972	5.171	9.954
Case converted to ch. 7	0.092	0.291	0.000	1.000
Case dismissed	0.103	0.306	0.000	1.000
Pre-packaged case	0.046	0.211	0.000	1.000
363 motion	0.299	0.460	0.000	1.000
Log of days in ch. 11	2.466	0.383	1.204	3.242
3+ professionals	0.609	0.491	0.000	1.000
OCP system	0.402	0.493	0.000	1.000
Interaction, OCP & 3+	0.287	0.455	0.000	1.000
Official committee	0.782	0.416	0.000	1.000
Claims agent	0.483	0.503	0.000	1.000
Case from SDNY	0.149	0.359	0.000	1.000
Delaware case	0.138	0.347	0.000	1.000
Highest hourly rate	555.908	185.696	215.000	950.000
Trustee	0.080	0.274	0.000	1.000
Examiner	0.034	0.184	0.000	1.000
Fee examiner	0.069	0.255	0.000	1.000

Std. Dev. not adjusted for clustering

Appendix 10B: Collinearity Diagnostics for Final Model on Table 10 (Big Case Sample)

Pairwise Correlation with Size		*VIF*	*Tolerance*
1.0000	Log of debtor size	4.500	0.222
-0.1183	Case converted to ch. 7	4.050	0.247
-0.0967	Case dismissed	2.790	0.359
0.2052*	Pre-packaged case	2.570	0.389
-0.1043	363 motion	2.520	0.397
-0.1419	Log of days in ch. 11	2.190	0.456
0.3066*	3+ professionals	2.190	0.458
0.4387*	OCP system	1.990	0.503
0.4158*	Interaction, OCP & 3+	1.920	0.522
0.2912*	Official committee	1.460	0.684
0.5523*	Claims agent	1.410	0.707
0.0068	Case from SDNY	1.330	0.750
0.1403	Delaware case	1.280	0.781
0.6043*	Highest hourly rate	1.270	0.784
-0.1550	Trustee	1.260	0.796
0.0526	Examiner	1.230	0.815
0.1991	Fee examiner	1.120	0.897
* $p < 0.05$	*Mean VIF*	2.060	

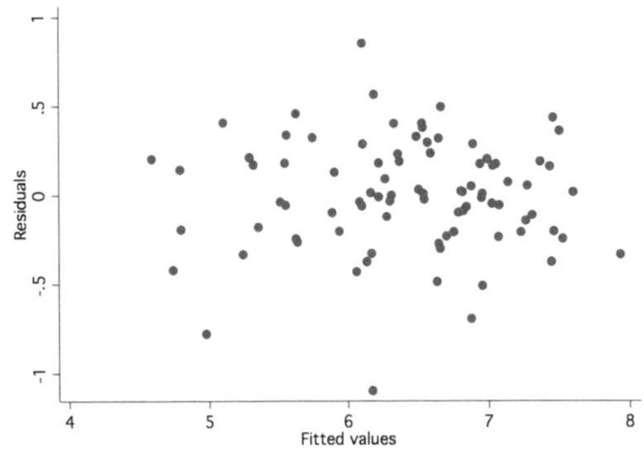

Appendix 10C: Residuals Plot for Final Mode in Table 10 (Big Case Dataset)

D. The Random Sample

Extending the model to the more typical, if less economically weighty, cases in the random sample is not simply a matter of changing datasets. First, about a third of cases in the random sample have no fee data. As Figure 11 reveals, this is not the result of slack record keeping in these smaller cases, but rather a reflection of a group of cases that fail to navigate through the chapter 11 system to a confirmed plan. Whether the professionals involved obtain any payment outside of the bankruptcy system is a matter of speculation, although some bankruptcy judges I spoke with indicated that such a payment was possible. But at the very least this suggests some substantial degree of risk is involved in chapter 11 practice, particularly with regard to smaller debtors. And if these cases are indeed ones that returned nothing to the professionals involved, this is not a instance of censoring or inflated zeros that should be addressed by the model itself. Rather, these are cases with "true" chapter 11 costs of zero, at least with regard to the kinds of costs measured by this study. To be sure, the costs of these cases may indirectly reflect in other cases in the sample, if the unpaid professionals account for the risk of non-payment in their rates.

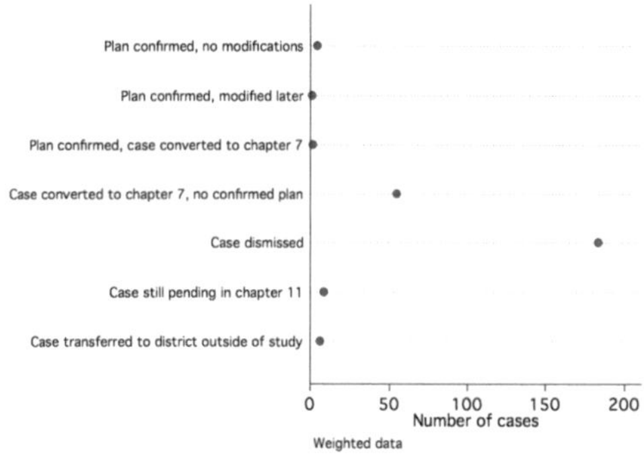

Figure 11: Case Outcomes with Missing Fee Data (Random Sample)

Omitting these cases from the analysis, the next challenge is to consider the different nature of the random dataset as compared to the big cases. For example, of the 655 cases that remain in the sample after elimination of the cases without fee data, less than 1% are prepackaged cases – indeed, there is only one prepackaged case in the random dataset. Fee examiners are equally rare. Indeed, examiners of any type are rare in this dataset, appearing in only 3% of cases.

Including a Delaware indicator is no longer justified, given that while more than 28% of the remaining cases are from New York,[153] only 7% are from Delaware. In a random sample of chapter 11 cases, Delaware becomes just another state.

Thus, I begin with the basic framework of the final model from Table 10, but change it in important ways suggested by the differences in the dataset described above. First, I simply omit the prepackaged case variable because inclusion would make the variable a proxy for the single prepackaged case in the sample. For similar reasons I omit the fee examiner, ordinary course professional, 363 sale, examiner and Delaware variables.[154]

The fee structure in the random dataset is also quite different. Lead counsel in this dataset have *top* hourly rates that range from $100 per hour to $950 per hour. Indeed, the *lowest* hourly rates in the largest cases are substantially higher than $100 – paralegals typically bill at a higher hourly rate. Thus I replace the "high rate" variable with a dummy variable that asks if lead debtor's counsel's highest hourly rate was above the median of $250 per hour for this dataset.[155]

This revised – "stripped down" – version of the prior big case model explains more than 79% of chapter 11 costs for this group of typical chapter 11 cases. It appears as Model 1 on Table 12.

153 See Table 12A at the end of the section for descriptive statistics for the cases used in the models.
154 Save for Delaware, which as noted represents 7% of the cases in the dataset, these variables all register positive responses in less than 5% of cases.
155 The mean hourly rate is $360.06.

Table 12: Models of Chapter 11 Costs (Random Dataset)

	(1) *Log of total case cost*	(2) *Log of total case cost*
Log of debtor size	0.380***	0.363***
	(0.0952)	(0.0795)
Case converted to chapter 7	-0.286***	-0.251**
	(0.0763)	(0.0729)
Case dismissed	-0.423***	-0.388***
	(0.0533)	(0.0575)
Trustee	0.471**	0.444***
	(0.144)	(0.114)
Log of days in chapter 11	0.448***	0.422***
	(0.108)	(0.0997)
3+ professionals	0.340***	0.370***
	(0.0871)	(0.0976)
Official committee	0.480***	0.359**
	(0.115)	(0.118)
Claims agent	0.716***	0.622***
	(0.0855)	(0.0868)
Highest hourly rate above median ($325)	0.386***	0.334***
	(0.0765)	(0.0738)
DIP Financing		0.130
		(0.104)
"First day" motions		0.201
		(0.111)
Secured debt over total debt		-0.0157
		(0.0714)
Constant	0.928	1.072
	(0.616)	(0.555)
Observations	335	335
R2	0.795	0.808
Adjusted *R2*	0.790	0.801

Robust standard errors in parentheses; se adjusted for clustering by district; mean VIF (model 2) = 1.50

* $p < 0.05$, ** $p < 0.01$, *** $p < 0.001$

I then introduce some new concepts, to better refine the model and capture the differences amongst the cases in the dataset. First, I hypothesized that there might be at least two types of chapter 11 cases lurking in the data: first, a case were the debtor's assets are of marginal value, and the goal is to get in and out of the process as cheaply as possible, and secondly a case where there is real value in conducting a more formal reorganization process. To distinguish between the two, I add a dummy variable that indicates whether the debtor obtained post-petition (i.e., DIP) financing, with the hypothesis that receipt of such financing would indicate the second type of case, or at least that the bank considered the debtor to be of the second type, and thus I would expect this variable to be positively correlated with chapter 11 costs.

I return to the question of case complexity and model the "elite" chapter 11 cases in this dataset with the variable that indicates whether first-day papers were filed in the case.[156] This variable should be positively related to cost, as it reflects debtors that require extra professional effort.[157]

Finally, I hypothesize that secured creditors might have a comparative advantage in these comparably smaller chapter 11 cases, in as much as they might be able to exercise greater oversight over the chapter 11 process given their greater legal rights,[158] and the tendency for secured creditors to be more consolidated as compared with the typically smaller unsecured creditors. This might lower costs. Thus, I enter the ratio of secured to total debt into the model, which I would predict should be negatively related to overall chapter 11 costs. The regression coefficient is negative, suggesting that such a cost saving effect indeed occurs.

This augmented model is shown as Model 2 on Table 12. It explains more than 80% of chapter 11 costs, across the full universe of chapter 11. But none of the new variables are independently significant and the change in R-squared from model 1 to model 2 is not significant.

The differences between these models and the big case models I have previously presented highlight the important distinctions that exist between the "average" chapter 11 case and the cases that absorb most of the time and attention of academics. The average chapter 11 case is not merely a smaller version of its better-known counterpart, rather it is a distinct subspecies of the reorganization process. This suggests several important avenues for further study.

For example, for jurisdictions that would like to adopt a chapter 11-like process, which version of chapter 11 should they adopt? More importantly, will jurisdictions without a tradition of judicial flexibility be able to realize the value of a system like chapter 11, or would they be better served by adopting distinct small and big business reorganization provisions? For example, chapter 11 seems to work well for larger firms because the bankruptcy courts are willing to approve procedures that modify the terms of the Bankruptcy Code. In other jurisdictions, courts might not be so willing to override the terms of a statute.

Note also that time and debtor size are significant factors in modeling the "average" chapter 11 case, whereas I previously found that time and, to a lesser degree, size were proxies for other factors that could be modeled when considering big chapter 11 cases. Do these differences suggest real differences between the

156 Mark A. McDermott, *Critical Vendor and Related Orders: Kmart and the Bankruptcy Abuse Prevention and Consumer Protection Act of 2005*, 14 AM. BANKR. INST. L. REV. 409 (2006).

157 This variable was not used in connection with Table 10 because of colinearity – indeed, almost perfect correlation – between the OCP variable and this variable.

158 In the United States, secured creditors are deemed to have a property right that is constitutionally protected. Thus, they have a right to "adequate protection" of the secured portion of their claim, and if the debtor fails to provide such protection the automatic stay will be lifted to allow the creditor to take the collateral. 11 U.S.C. §§ 361, 362(d), 506. Unsecured creditors have no such rights under federal law, by virtue of the constitutional bankruptcy power.

datasets? For example, the smaller law firms working on the "average" chapter 11 case may have less ability to adjust the staffing of a case to accommodate a particular timeframe, making case length a factor in cost. Or do the differences simply reflect the need for further, fine-grain study of the world of smaller chapter 11 cases?

Appendix 12A: Descriptive Statistics for Models (Random Dataset)

Number of obs. = 335	*Mean*	*Std. Dev.*	*Min*	*Max*
Dependent (Log of total costs)	4.889	0.879	2.778	7.596
Log of debtor size	6.387	0.665	4.680	9.005
Case converted to chapter 7	0.199	0.400	0.000	1.000
Case dismissed	0.309	0.463	0.000	1.000
Trustee	0.077	0.267	0.000	1.000
Log of days in chapter 11	2.489	0.304	1.176	3.017
3+ professionals	0.155	0.362	0.000	1.000
Official committee	0.337	0.473	0.000	1.000
Claims agent	0.094	0.292	0.000	1.000
Highest hourly rate above median ($250)	0.755	0.431	0.000	1.000
DIP Financing	0.260	0.439	0.000	1.000
"First day" motions	0.341	0.475	0.000	1.000
Secured Debt over total debt	0.532	0.329	0.000	1.000

Weighted data; std. dev. not adjusted for clustering

Summary

This chapter begins by examining the cost associated with the big case dataset. In this dataset, the average case incurred over $8.4 million ($3.7 million median) in total professional costs. Alternatively stated, the debtors in this dataset incurred almost $34,000 ($11,795) per day in chapter 11 – although costs are not incurred in a uniform manner.

The chapter then develops a model of chapter 11 costs with respect to the large corporate debtors. This model challenges several key assumptions about the way chapter 11 works, and how chapter 11 costs are incurred.

Cases filed in Delaware appear to be less expensive than comparable cases filed elsewhere, while time spent in chapter 11 is not related to the amount of professional costs incurred. Instead, complexity and debtor size, which I argue are distinct concepts, provide the most important determinates of cost in these large cases.

I also develop a model of chapter 11 costs with regard to a random sample of chapter 11 debtors. Importantly, the substantial differences between the two datasets in terms of what factors explain cost highlight the distinct nature of chapter 11 as experienced by large and small debtors.

Time spent in chapter 11 and debtor size are significant factors in modeling the "average" chapter 11 case, whereas I previously found that time and, to a lesser degree, size were proxies for other factors that could be modeled when considering big chapter 11 cases. Differences abound.

V The Bankruptcy Attorneys

In a large chapter 11 case, the single biggest source of costs are the bankruptcy attorneys, or, more precisely, their law firms. The lead debtor's counsel is the key actor in the case, coordinating the work of all other debtor professionals while also handling the core legal work of the case.[159] The lead committee's counsel plays a similar role with regard to the unsecured creditors, and the two law firms together contribute to the overall cost of a case to such a degree that they warrant separate consideration. Because committees, and lead and local counsel, are issues primarily in big case, this chapter focuses solely on the big case dataset.

A. Measuring the Role of Lead Attorneys

In the United States, bankruptcy counsel often comes as a pair of law firms. This is because lawyers are licensed on a state-by-state basis, and large corporate debtors often hire bankruptcy counsel from a city other than where their case will be filed. The most well-known example of this involves cases filed in Delaware by law firms headquartered in one of the three largest cities in the United States.[160] In such a case the debtor would also have to hire "local counsel," that is a law firm based in Delaware.[161]

Table 13A shows the breakdown between these two costs for debtor's counsel. The number of "local counsel" entries is substantially smaller than lead counsel, because all cases must have lead debtor's counsel, but not all cases need have local counsel. For example, a case filed in San Francisco by a California law firm, even one located 500 miles (800 km) away in San Diego, will not have local counsel.

159 As used in this chapter, lead counsel is typically a law firm, rather than any individual lawyer.

160 New York, Los Angeles and Chicago, respectively.

161 One notable exception involves Skadden, Arps, a large New York-based law firm with an office in Wilmington, Delaware. The Delaware office of the firm acts as the firm's "local counsel." Skadden, Arps is among the three leading debtor law firms in the United States – a group that also includes Weil, Gotshal and Kirkland & Ellis. Stephen J. Lubben, *Choosing Corporate Bankruptcy Counsel*, 12 Am. Bankr. Inst. L. Rev. 391 (2006).

Table 13A: Cost of Debtor's Bankruptcy Counsel

	Obs	Mean	Std. Dev.	Median	Min	Max
Debtor's counsel (total)	91	$2,809,579.00	$6,315,713.00	$1,194,498.00	$29,698.79	$55,100,000.00
Debtor's counsel (lead)	91	$2,540,013.00	$5,657,659.00	$1,056,852.00	$29,698.79	$49,300,000.00
Debtor's counsel (lead) -- no prepacks	87	$2,637,200.00	$5,768,915.00	$1,094,877.00	$29,698.79	$49,300,000.00
Debtor's counsel (local)	31	$791,305.70	$1,237,460.00	$444,687.60	$10,076.50	$5,801,208.00

As shown on the Table, the bulk of debtor's counsel cost comes from the lead debtor's counsel, which is to be expected. Local counsel is primarily tasked with reviewing pleading generated by lead counsel for compliance with local law. I include lead counsel both with and without the prepackaged cases in the sample, to consider the effects of any time-shifting of fees into the pre-bankruptcy period in the prepackaged cases. Table 13A shows the effects of this by comparing lead debtor's counsel costs for prepackaged cases against the traditional cases. Although the number of prepackaged cases is very small, the difference is significant (p=0.0006). These results suggest the need to account for this factor in subsequent models.

Table 13B: Lead Debtor's Counsel Costs by Case Type

	Obs	Mean	Std. Err.	Std. Dev.	[95% Conf.	Interval]
Prepackaged	4	$426,205.10	$32,214.08	$64,428.16	$323,685.50	$528,724.60
Traditional	87	$2,637,200.00	$618,492.60	$5,768,915.00	$1,407,677.00	$3,866,722.00
Combined	91	$2,540,013.00	$593,083.80	$5,657,659.00	$1,361,749.00	$3,718,278.00

Committee counsel fees present the same issue of lead and local counsel, with the additional wrinkle that a case may have more than one committee. Prepackaged cases play less of a role here, because committees are frequently "unofficial" in prepackaged cases, preferring to be paid before the case is filed and thus avoid court oversight. Table 14 presents the lead and local counsel information for the cases in the dataset, along with the specific information for the creditor's committee in the case.[162] The difference between these figures and the overall figures represents the effects of additional committees, such as those representing equity, employees, trade creditors or subordinated bondholders. Average lead debtor's counsel is about twice lead committee's counsel, although there are obviously

162 There are two fewer creditors committees than cases with committees, as two cases had "unofficial" or "ad hoc" bondholders committees along with official equity committees. That is, two cases had some form of committee, but not an official committee of unsecured creditors.

some cases without committees.[163] This somewhat conflicts with Lynn LoPucki's findings that debtor lead attorneys earned four times as much as lead creditor's counsel, based on a non-random sample of 74 chapter 11 cases filed just before the cases in this study, that is, between 1998 and 2003.[164]

Table 14: Cost of Committee Bankruptcy Counsel

	Obs	*Mean*	*Std. Dev.*	*Median*	*Min*	*Max*
Committee counsel (total)	72	$1,288,754.00	$1,584,375.00	$630,421.30	$17,054.65	$9,050,715.00
Committee counsel (lead)	72	$1,195,763.00	$1,544,186.00	$606,360.80	$17,054.65	$8,999,914.00
Unsecured creditors committee only (lead)	70	$1,104,953.00	$1,423,621.00	$606,360.80	$17,054.65	$8,999,914.00
Committee counsel (local)	24	$278,974.90	$304,506.50	$126,228.30	$9,180.89	$1,050,523.00
Unsecured creditors committee only (local)	23	$245,429.40	$262,114.50	$82,761.41	$9,180.89	$1,008,527.00

Here we see that lead counsel for the primary creditors' committee is the most substantial piece of committee counsel costs, and between the two tables it is apparent that lead counsel is the biggest overall component of bankruptcy counsel costs. The table also indicates that the first committee – the unsecured creditors committee – is the primary committee-related expense, there being but a slight difference between the average lead counsel cost for this committee and all committees.

The relationship between these costs and the overall cost of chapter 11 is illustrated in Figure 15.[165] In the broader universe of cases with committees, whether or not there is local counsel, debtor and committee counsel combine to account for almost half of the total cost of a chapter 11 case. It is also clear that lead counsel for both debtor and committee is the predominant source of counsel-related expense.

163 Debtor's counsel costs are 2.7 times committee counsel costs if the analysis is limited to those cases with committees.

164 Lynn M. LoPucki & Joseph W. Doherty, *Rise of the Financial Advisors: An Empirical Study of the Division of Professional Fees in Large Bankruptcies*, 82 Am. Bankr. L. J. 141 (2008) [hereinafter, "LoPucki (2008)"].

165 Note that prepackaged cases are excluded from this graph.

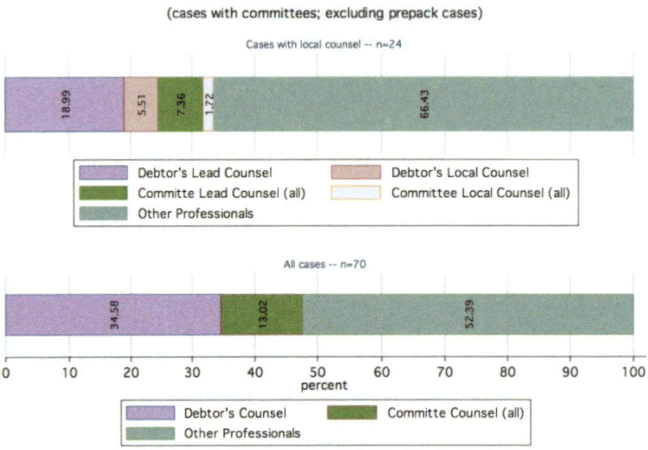

Figure 15: Mean Counsel Costs as Portion of Overall Cost

Figure 16 shows the national market that exists for lead bankruptcy counsel. While Delaware is often the focus of this discussion, the chart makes clear that debtors often file chapter 11 cases with the assistance of out of state counsel and Delaware is just the most publicized example of a larger phenomenon. Not surprisingly, New York law firms are the most likely to work on out of state matters, but firms from other cities, big and small, also show a willingness to cross state lines.[166] Combined with law firms from geographically large states like California and Texas, who seem to practice in judicial districts outside their own[167] – like Los Angeles law firms filing cases in the Northern District of California – this Figure shows that big corporate debtors can consider a broad range of law firms when approaching chapter 11.

As with general studies of chapter 11 costs, counsel costs show evidence of economies of scale. Table 17 shows that the very largest cases incurred much lower counsel costs as a percentage of overall size.[168]

166 The "home city" data in Figure 16 comes from the first three digits of the ZIP code found on the law firms' retention application. http://pe.usps.com/text/dmm300/L002.htm.

167 By way of comparison, California and Texas each comprise more than 150,000 square miles (more than 241,000 sq. km), whereas Poland is about 120,000 square miles. (more than 193,000 sq. km). Texas is geographically larger than any nation in the EU, and California is larger than any EU country save France.

168 The number of observations on this table differ from earlier tables because of missing debtor size data.

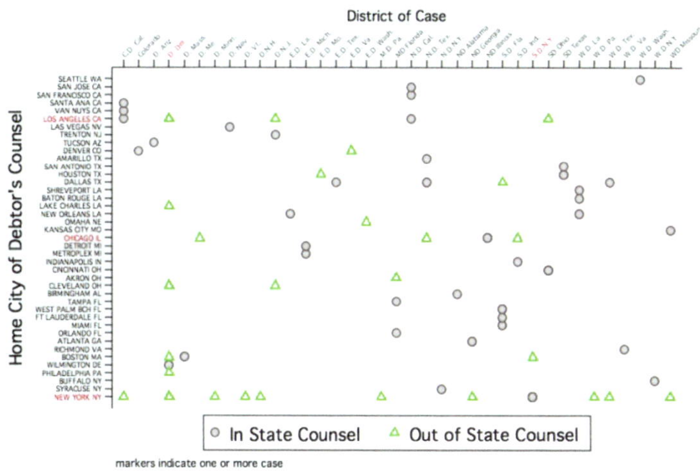

Figure 16: Case location vs. Counsel Location

Table 17: Standardized Counsel Costs by Size Quartiles

	Mean	*Std. Err.*	*[95% Conf.*	*Interval]*
Debtor counsel over size (n=89)				
(smallest) 1	0.049	0.013	0.023	0.074
2	0.037	0.006	0.024	0.049
3	0.010	0.001	0.007	0.013
4	0.008	0.003	0.002	0.014
Lead debtor counsel over size (n=89)				
(smallest) 1	0.048	0.013	0.022	0.074
2	0.034	0.006	0.022	0.045
3	0.009	0.001	0.006	0.012
4	0.007	0.003	0.002	0.013
Committee counsel over size (n=69)				
(smallest) 1	0.029	0.008	0.013	0.044
2	0.015	0.002	0.010	0.020
3	0.005	0.001	0.003	0.007
4	0.003	0.001	0.001	0.005
Lead committee counsel over size (1st comm.) (n=69)				
(smallest) 1	0.028	0.007	0.013	0.043
2	0.014	0.002	0.010	0.019
3	0.005	0.001	0.003	0.006
4	0.003	0.001	0.001	0.005

B. Modeling the Cost of Debtor Attorneys

Given the apparent scale relationship between bankruptcy counsel costs and debtor size, a regression model offers the most accurate way to estimate the expected amount that a debtor will pay to bankruptcy attorneys during a chapter 11 case. I begin by modeling the cost of debtor's lead counsel, the biggest single piece of counsel costs, before looking at committee costs.

Save for Lubben (2008), which offered some basic descriptive statistics on the breakdown of counsel costs, LoPucki (2008) is the only prior study to consider counsel costs distinct from overall chapter 11 costs. LoPucki and his co-author studied 74 debtors, all of which were publicly traded companies that filed between 1998 and 2003. They used the following factors in their model, which explained 83% of the variance in lead debtor's counsel costs for the cases in their sample:

Size (natural log of assets)
Time (natural log of days in chapter 11)
Number of debtor law firms (natural log)
Whether the case was filed in New York or Delaware (two dummy variables)
A trend variable (to capture the multi-year nature of the sample)
Whether the lead debtor's counsel was Skadden, Arps[169]

The authors found that size, time, and the presence of Skadden, Arps were all positively related to the cost of the debtor's lead bankruptcy attorneys ($p<0.01$). The number of law firms was significant only when measured at a lower standard ($p=0.10$). They concluded "Skadden Arps representation cost more in these cases because Skadden, Arps billed more hours."

I begin by testing this model with my dataset. I omit the trend variable, which is inapplicable as all of the cases in my dataset were filed in 2004. Number of law firms is modeled by a dummy that indicates if the case had local counsel.[170] The results appear on Table 18.

Size, time and Skadden, Arps are the significant factors in this model. The overall R-squared is relatively low, suggesting that either the broader nature of the present dataset, including both public and private companies, or the difference in years studied limit the generalizability of the LoPucki model.

169 Skadden, Arps, Slate, Meagher & Flom LLP, a large New York based corporate law firm. http://www.skadden.com/ The author was employed by this firm before entering academia in 2002.

170 This is slightly under inclusive of what is modeled in LoPucki (2008), since their variable also included foreign bankruptcy attorneys paid out of the U.S. bankruptcy estate. For example, if the debtor filed a parallel proceeding in Canada, and paid the professionals out of the United States entity, this would have been included. In my dataset, these professionals would appear as "additional professionals."

Table 18: LoPucki Model of Lead Debtor's Counsel Costs (Big Case Dataset)

	(1) *Log of debtor lead bankruptcy counsel costs*
Log of debtor size	0.408***
	(0.110)
Log of days in chapter 11	0.430*
	(0.191)
Local counsel in this case	0.180
	(0.143)
Delaware case	-0.0719
	(0.132)
Case from SDNY	0.223
	(0.145)
Lead debtor's counsel was Skadden, Arps	0.414*
	(0.160)
Constant	1.529
	(1.185)
Observations	89
$R2$	0.505

Robust standard errors in parentheses; based on Model III, Figure 6 of LoPucki (2008)
* $p < 0.05$, ** $p < 0.01$, *** $p < 0.001$

Thus on Table 19 I begin to develop my own model. In the first model I consider the bivariate relationship between debtor size and lead counsel cost. Theory would suggest that this relationship should be positive, but it should also diminish in importance as the model becomes more specific.

In the second model I enter variables that capture case conditions that require the debtor's lead counsel to interact with other professionals in the case, possibly increasing costs. In particular I include dummy variables to indicate if a committee was appointed and if the debtor retained several (three) additional professionals other than lead and local bankruptcy counsel. Appointment of an examiner is also included in this model. At this stage I also include a dummy variable that indicates whether the case is prepackaged, since the model only considers post-petition fees, which suggests that pre-petition cases should appear to incur lower attorneys' fees. The first three variables should be positively associated with cost, while the prepackaged case variable should be inversely related to cost.

In the next model I introduce the use of an ordinary course professional (OCP) system and a claims agent as indicators of case complexity. These variables should be positively related to counsel costs. The OCP system variable not only captures complexity itself, but also the reality that the administration of an OCP system typically falls on the lead debtor's counsel.

In the fourth model I consider the direct effect of the lead counsel's hourly rates by adding the highest hourly rate charged by debtor's lead counsel. This variable not only captures the obvious effect of this top rate, but also indicates the overall scale of bankruptcy counsel's rate structure. This variable should have a positive relationship with cost.

The fifth model examines new factors that might specifically influence lead debtor's counsel cost. First I input a dummy variable that captures if the debtor's lead counsel was from out of state, relative to the district where the case was filed. This not only captures the information contained in the "local counsel" variable used in connection with the LoPucki model, but it also captures situations where an out of state law firm was able to file without local counsel because at least one member of the firm was admitted to the bar of the state where the case was filed. Out of state location should be associated, at the very least, with higher travel expense, and thus I hypothesize that this variable should have a positive effect on cost. Next I input a variable that indicates if the debtor's lead law firm was headquartered in New York, reflecting the common belief that New York law firms are more expensive than firms from other cities.

Given that Figure 16 has already shown that New York firms often work out of state, I also include an interaction term to indicate the joint effect of a New York firm working out of state. The common perception of New York law firms suggests that both of these variables should have a positive coefficient. On the other hand, these same firms are likely to be amongst the most experienced, which may point the other direction. LoPucki (2008) did not find any effect from retaining New York counsel or out of state counsel.

The final model replaces these three variables with the two variables that were significant in the LoPucki model on Table 18 – namely, retention of Skadden and time spent in chapter 11. Rather than an extension of the prior model, this is instead an alternative model that allows for some consideration of the robustness of the key results shown on Table 19.

The immediate take-away from Table 19 is that neither the LoPucki factors nor the out of state and New York factors add much to this model, in terms increasing the amount of variance explained. Either Model 5 or 6 is but a slight improvement from Model 4, which explains almost 77% of the total variance in costs of lead debtor's counsel. Importantly, the claims made in LoPucki (2008) regarding Skadden, Arps are not born out in a more completely specified model, suggesting that the Skadden variable was acting as a proxy for case complexity or other factors on Table 18.

The keys to explaining the costs associated with lead debtor's counsel appear to be factors that increase the number of professionals counsel has to interact with (appointment of an examiner, retention of additional professionals, use of an OCP motion) and the rate structure, with the top hourly rate positively associated with cost.

Table 19: Models of Lead Debtor's Counsel Costs (Big Case Dataset)

	(1) *Log of debtor lead bankruptcy counsel costs*	(2) *Log of debtor lead bankruptcy counsel costs*	(3) *Log of debtor lead bankruptcy counsel costs*	(4) *Log of debtor lead bankruptcy counsel costs*	(5) *Log of debtor lead bankruptcy counsel costs*	(6) *Log of debtor lead bankruptcy counsel costs*
Log of debtor size	0.437***	0.379***	0.253*	0.178	0.181	0.178
	(0.0959)	(0.0916)	(0.0982)	(0.0974)	(0.102)	(0.109)
3+ Professionals		0.429**	0.381***	0.385***	0.390***	0.360***
		(0.132)	(0.0965)	(0.0817)	(0.0882)	(0.0980)
Official comm		0.329*	0.193	0.226	0.229	0.183
		(0.139)	(0.146)	(0.131)	(0.145)	(0.133)
Examiner		0.507***	0.586**	0.497**	0.539**	0.466*
		(0.0877)	(0.172)	(0.157)	(0.172)	(0.183)
Pre-packaged		-0.375	-0.478*	-0.558*	-0.569*	-0.445
		(0.235)	(0.223)	(0.239)	(0.247)	(0.288)
Claims agent			0.295*	0.0588	0.0499	0.0791
			(0.116)	(0.0829)	(0.0799)	(0.0985)
OCP motion			0.339**	0.245**	0.238**	0.247**
			(0.104)	(0.0856)	(0.0863)	(0.0895)
Top hourly rate				0.00130**	0.00134**	0.00126**
				(0.000359)	(0.000392)	(0.000391)
Out of state firm					0.0187	
					(0.110)	
New York firm					0.0396	
					(0.0864)	
NY & out of state					-0.125	
					(0.169)	
Log days in ch. 11						0.135
						(0.189)
Skadden retained						0.118
						(0.181)
Constant	2.490**	2.419***	3.276***	3.276***	3.235***	2.992**
	(0.745)	(0.629)	(0.639)	(0.550)	(0.581)	(0.910)
Observations	83	83	83	83	83	83
*R*2	0.380	0.616***	0.716**	0.767***	0.769	0.772

Robust standard errors in parentheses; se adjusted for clustering by district; mean VIF (Model 5) 2.03, (Model 6) 1.71

** $p < 0.05$, ** $p < 0.01$, *** $p < 0.001$*

As predicted, debtor size declines in importance as the models become more fully specified – in Model 4 debtor size is no longer significant (p=0.053).

Table 20 then examines the models developed in connection with debtor's lead counsel in connection with the overall cost of debtor's counsel – that is, lead and local counsel combined.

Table 20: Models of Total Debtor's Counsel Costs (Big Case Dataset)

	(1) *Log of lead and local debtor's counsel costs*	*(2)* *Log of lead and local debtor's counsel costs*
Log of debtor size	0.184	0.176
	(0.0987)	(0.102)
3+ professionals	0.368***	0.381***
	(0.0813)	(0.0893)
Official committee	0.227	0.227
	(0.130)	(0.143)
Examiner	0.502**	0.532**
	(0.168)	(0.184)
Pre-packaged case	-0.570*	-0.570*
	(0.246)	(0.241)
Claims agent	0.0795	0.0554
	(0.0782)	(0.0750)
OCP motion	0.269**	0.259**
	(0.0757)	(0.0731)
Top hourly rate	0.00133***	0.00135**
	(0.000361)	(0.000386)
Out of state law firm		0.106
		(0.101)
New York law firm		0.0254
		(0.0838)
NY and out of state		-0.149
		(0.161)
Constant	3.241***	3.270***
	(0.555)	(0.581)
Observations	83	83
R2	0.784	0.788

Robust standard errors in parentheses; se adjusted for clustering by district; mean VIF (model 2) = 2.03

* $p < 0.05$, ** $p < 0.01$, *** $p < 0.001$

Again we see that New York firms and out of state law firms contribute very little to understanding the overall cost of a debtor's bankruptcy attorneys.[171] Instead the key factors are those that increase the number of parties counsel has to communicate with and the rate structure of the lead law firm.

171 In a third model, which I don't show, I examined the retention of Skadden, Arps. The variable was not significant (p=0.573) and the model little changed (R-squared = 0.79).

C. Modeling the Cost of Committee Attorneys

The costs of committee counsel should involve somewhat different factors, inasmuch as committee counsel is conditional on the existence of debtor counsel. And the variables that measure the number of additional parties to the case should have less influence here, as the committee is typically not the central party to these interactions.

Modeling committee counsel costs also presents a special challenge because there can be multiple committees within a single case, but the declining number of committees after the first does not leave sufficient numbers for separate analysis. To address this problem, I focus my efforts on lead counsel for the first committee appointed in the cases

This section represents the first effort to model committee counsel fees, as LoPucki (2008) focused solely on debtor-retained attorneys.

Model 1 on Table 20 begins with some basic factors taken from the prior debtor counsel models. Debtor size and a proxy for complexity, appointment of a claims agent, are entered at this point. Both should be positively related to the cost of lead committee counsel. I do not use OCP motions in this model, because the effects of such motions should be felt on the debtor side of the case. As will be seen, neither variable is ultimately significant.

In Model 2, I account for the hourly rate structure of lead committee counsel by including the lead law firm's highest hourly rate. This variable should also be positively related to cost. This variable is significant in both Models 2 and 3.

In the third model I consider the parties that committee counsel might have to interact with, beyond the debtor. In particular, I enter variables that indicate if there is an additional committee, if there is a financial advisor in the case (retained by any party to the case),[172] and if there is an examiner. All should positively relate to cost, and all are ultimately significant in Model 3.

In the fourth and final model I examine the idea that committee counsel costs might be largely incurred in reaction to debtor counsel costs. The more active debtor's counsel is in the case, the more the committee's counsel will expend effort in monitoring and engaging with that activity. Thus, I include the log of the total fees incurred by debtor's counsel, including both lead and local counsel.[173] The variable is positive and significant ($p<0.001$).

172 Financial advisors are used here in place of the "additional professional" variable used with regard to debtor's attorneys, as some of the additional professionals may not work on bankruptcy matters, and thus would have no reason to interact with the committee.

173 The potential reverse causation problems are discussed, *infra* Table 22.

Table 21: Models of Total Committee Counsel Costs (Big Case Dataset)

	(1) Log of total committee lead bankruptcy counsel costs (first comm)	(2) Log of total committee lead bankruptcy counsel costs (first comm)	(3) Log of total committee lead bankruptcy counsel costs (first comm)	(4) Log of total committee lead bankruptcy counsel costs (first comm)
Log debtor size	0.245	0.154	0.00576	-0.0175
	(0.127)	(0.120)	(0.0976)	(0.0414)
Claims agent	0.371	0.202	0.106	-0.0727
	(0.187)	(0.159)	(0.117)	(0.103)
Highest rate		0.00145**	0.00169***	0.000983*
		(0.000408)	(0.000361)	(0.000376)
2d Committee			0.322*	-0.0450
			(0.138)	(0.154)
F. advisor			0.369**	0.0873
			(0.124)	(0.102)
Examiner			0.582***	0.305
			(0.139)	(0.191)
Log D. counsel				0.656***
				(0.117)
Constant	3.556***	3.577***	4.323***	1.261
	(0.939)	(0.798)	(0.642)	(0.715)
Observations	61	61	61	61
$R2$	0.364	0.489***	0.662***	0.814***

Robust standard errors in parentheses; se adjusted for clustering by district; mean VIF (model 4) = 1.88

$* p < 0.05$, $** p < 0.01$, $*** p < 0.001$

Consistent with the theory that committee counsel costs are highly influenced by the debtor and its counsel's actions, Model 4 shows that debtor counsel fees are the most important factor in predicting lead committee counsel fees. Rate structure, represented by the highest hourly rate, is the only other significant factor in this model. Indeed, a model comprised of only these two independent variables (not shown) achieves an R-squared of 76.44%.

But there is an obvious reverse causality issue in the final model. Namely, it seems equally plausible – perhaps even more plausible, for a former debtor's attorney like myself – that it might be committee counsel costs that are driving debtor's counsel costs. Committee counsel might act as a kind of "back seat driver," causing debtor's counsel to expend extra effort. Indeed, my models of debtor counsel cost were based on a subtler version of this argument, when I included appointment of a committee as a factor that would increase the number of parties counsel must interact with. And if this is not a pure case of reverse causality, there might well be at least some degree of feedback, so that the debtor and committee counsel become self-reinforcing. If either of these factors are at play, the conclusions drawn from Model 4 must be considered with care.

To examine this specific issue, I revisit Model 4 on table 21, replacing the debtor counsel fee variable with the log of the bankruptcy-related fees paid before commencement of the case, as reported on the debtor's statement of financial affairs (SOFA). Since the committee is not appointed until after the case is filed, these pre-bankruptcy fees are not influenced by the actions of the committee counsel, yet the pre-bankruptcy and debtor counsel cost variables are highly correlated (0.7246). In short, pre-bankruptcy fees act as a proxy for debtor counsel fees, without the interpretive conundrum.

But the combined effect of cases without committees and cases with missing SOFAs leaves but 39 cases, a very small number to work with in a multivariate regression. To overcome this problem I impute the missing values for this variable. I use the ICE module for Stata.[174] This software creates multiple imputed datasets for a dataset with missing values – in this case I created 15 datasets with values imputed for missing values. The imputations are created using a Bayesian approach, based on the information available in the dataset and are created to retain the covariance structure of the sample, while taking advantage of the most information possible. For comparative purposes, the non-imputed version of the same model is shown in the shaded column on Table 22.

Table 22: Imputed Model of Total Committee Counsel Costs

	(1) *Log of total committee lead bankruptcy counsel costs (first comm)*	*No imputed data*
Log of debtor size	0.00508	-0.0531
	(0.0993)	(0.146)
Claims agent	0.112	0.0659
	(0.123)	(0.190)
Highest hourly rate	0.00169***	0.00158*
	(0.000375)	(0.000733)
2d committee	0.318	0.348
	(0.156)	(0.185)
Financial advisor	0.366**	0.218
	(0.129)	(0.228)
Examiner	0.586***	0.290***
	(0.140)	(0.0686)
Log, pre-bankruptcy costs	0.00000686	0.0964
	(0.0466)	(0.189)
Constant	4.331***	4.438***
	(0.656)	(0.821)
Observations	**62**	**39**
R2	0.664	0.622

Robust standard errors in parentheses; se adjusted for clustering by district; Mean VIF 1.44
** $p < 0.05$, ** $p < 0.01$, *** $p < 0.001$*

174 Patrick Royston, *Multiple Imputation Of Missing Values: Update Of ICE*, 15 STATA J. 527 (2005).

This method does not attempt to estimate the exact values that are missing but instead to provide a less biased information matrix than would occur from deleting cases with any missing data through listwise deletion. Creating several imputed datasets and combining the results of the analysis with each set is considered one of the best approaches to handling missing data, and far superior to single imputation methods that artificially reduce standard errors and increase the risk of falsely concluding a significant association when none exists.[175]

Table 22 displays the results, and strongly suggests that costs flow in the opposite direction as hypothesized in connection with Table 21. Namely since the pre-bankruptcy cost variable is not significant, Table 22 suggests that it is committee counsel that is driving debtor counsel costs. The debtor reacts to the committee.

Accordingly, Model 4 on Table 21 should be discarded and Model 3 viewed as the better method of estimating committee counsel costs. Accordingly, counsel's top hourly rate and measure of the number of parties that the committee interacts with are the key determinants of committee counsel costs. Notably, debtor size is again not a significant determinant.

Summary

Counsel costs are the most significant single component of overall chapter 11 costs, making up almost half of the total cost of a chapter 11 case.

Importantly, bankruptcy counsel for large debtors compete in a nationwide market in the United States. While Delaware is often the focus of this discussion, the chapter makes clear that debtors often file chapter 11 cases with the assistance of out of state counsel and Delaware is just the most publicized example of a larger phenomenon.

The regression models in this chapter show that the key factor in counsel costs is the size of the web of parties engaged in a chapter 11 case. The debtor's lead bankruptcy counsel stands in the middle of this web, and the more parties they have to interact with the greater the amount the debtor will have to pay to attorneys in its case. Committee counsel can particularly influence the size of debtor counsel costs.

175 J. L. Schafer & J.W. Graham, *Missing Data: Our View Of The State Of The Art*, 7 Psychological Methods 147, 170 (2002).

VI Financial Advisors & Turnaround Consultants

It has been observed that large chapter 11 cases have become increasingly "professionalized."[176] In particular, while once debtor's counsel might have handled the bulk of the reorganization, the debtor now routinely retains specialized professionals to address specific aspects of the case.

Among the most controversial of these non-legal professionals have been the financial advisors, as they often earn transaction fees based on either the sale or reorganization of the debtor.[177] Specifically, financial advisors are typically compensated with a combination of flat monthly fees and outcome contingent transactional fees, and thus fit uneasily into the American chapter 11 system, which is largely dominated by lawyers, and former lawyers acting as judges, both of whom are most accustomed to billing hourly rates plus expenses.[178]

Bankruptcy financial advisors come in two broad types. First there are the investment banker-type advisors, who either help market (i.e. find a buyer for) the debtor or advise the debtor on business changes going forward.[179] Alternatively, if retained by a committee they provide advice about the debtor's business prospects and the financial terms of the proposed plan. Second there are the accounting firms that act as financial advisors. They typically provide similar business advice to either the debtor or the committee that retains them, but are less likely to engage in direct efforts to sell the debtor. In addition, both types of financial advisor typically present valuation evidence at the hearing to consider a reorganization plan for the debtor.[180]

---

176 Jo Ann Brighton et al., *For Better Or Worse: Chapter 11 In The Post-BAPCPA Downturn*, 7 DePaul Bus. & Com. L.J. 555, 578 (2009).

177 http://www.bloomberg.com/apps/news?pid=20601087&sid=apzbxu6eOxik. *See* In re Hillsborough Holdings Corp., 125 B.R. 837 (Bankr. M.D. Fla. 1991).

178 Michael L. Cook & Stephen J. Lubben, *Retention, Payment, Ethical And Other Obstacles For Non-Legal Professionals In Chapter 11 Reorganizations*, 66 PLI/NY 175 (1999) ("Courts throughout the country differ in their views of non-legal professionals. Retention arrangements that are routinely approved in Manhattan and Wilmington may be met with skepticism, if not outright hostility, in Los Angeles, Denver, or Tampa.").

179 Until 2005, these firms were typically not the large, well-known American investment banks, as the Bankruptcy Code expressly precluded retention of an investment banker that had been an underwriter for the debtor's securities. In addition, it should be noted that financial advisors retained in chapter 11 cases only rarely underwrite securities offerings, so some would argue they are not actually "investment bankers."

180 For example, in all cases the debtor is required to prove that creditors are receiving at least as much as they would in a hypothetical chapter 7 liquidation. 11 U.S.C. §1129(a)(7). This requires the creation of a "liquidation analysis" and presentation of the same at the hearing. *See* Peter V. Pantaleo & Barry W. Ridings, *Reorganization Value*, 51 Bus. Law 419 (1996).

Somewhat related to the financial advisors are the turnaround consultants.[181] These are professionals retained by the debtor. Like financial advisors, they provide business advice to the debtor – indeed, some of the same firms act as financial advisors when retained by a committee. But these turnaround consultants typically become more involved in the direct management of the debtor, often taking positions within the senior management of the debtor. In some instances, the retention of these firms is mandated by a senior lender or the lead lender for the group of banks in the debtor's secured credit facility. Appointment of a turnaround firm and a member of that firm as "chief restructuring officer" is sometimes the price for obtaining additional financing during a chapter 11 case.[182] In other cases, turnaround firms, despite their hopeful names, provide the management of a remnant debtor following an asset sale, liquidating unsold assets, and working toward a plan that will distribute the sale proceeds.

There are 33 turnaround firms retained in the present dataset, across 30 chapter 11 cases. That is, in three cases debtors retained two turnaround firms, while 27 debtors retained a single turnaround firm. 33 fee applications is often an insufficient number to analyze separately, but given the somewhat unique role these professionals play, it warrants accounting for their presence when considering the topic of financial advisors, broadly defined.

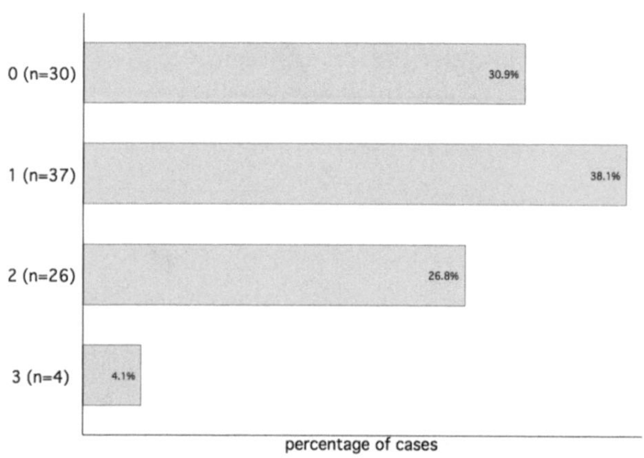

Figure 24: Number of Debtor Financial Advisors & Turnaround Consultants

181 The only other study of financial advisors in chapter 11 includes turnaround consultants among its definition of financial advisors. Lynn M. LoPucki & Joseph W. Doherty, *Rise of the Financial Advisors: An Empirical Study of the Division of Professional Fees in Large Bankruptcies*, 82 Am. Bankr. L. J. 141 (2008) [hereinafter, "LoPucki (2008)"].

182 Douglas G. Baird & Robert K. Rasmussen, *Private Debt and the Missing Lever of Corporate Governance*, 154 U. Pa. L. Rev. 1209, 1229 (2006).

A. Prevalence and Cost of Financial Advisors

As shown on Figure 24, almost 70% of the debtors, or 67 of 97 debtors, in the dataset retain at least one financial advisor or turnaround consultant, and an almost equal number retain more than one. Eleven debtors retained a turnaround consultant but no financial advisor.

In the dataset, 74 of the 97 cases have at least one committee. In 57 of these cases the committees retained at least one financial advisor.

Table 25 shows the relationship between retention of financial advisors by the debtor and its committees. Note that zero committee retentions on this table can either mean there was no committee, which happened in 22 cases, or the committee retained no financial advisors, which happened in 18 cases, yielding the 40 total cases seen on the Table. Other than no financial advisors or turnaround consultants in the case whatsoever, the next most likely outcome is for the debtor and committee to each retain one financial advisor or turnaround consultant, followed closely by one committee retention and two debtor retentions.

Table 25: Number of Financial Advisors & Turnaround Consultants

	Retained by committees in case			
Retained by debtor in case	0	1	2	*Total*
0	24	6	0	30
1	12	22	3	37
2	4	19	3	26
3	0	2	2	4
Total	*40*	*49*	*8*	*97*

In eleven cases there was more than one committee appointed. In all of these cases the committees retained at least one financial advisor, and in six cases they retained two – most often with each committee retaining its own financial advisor. Multiple retentions of financial advisors by debtors do not seem to turn on the number of committees. For example, there are 26 cases where the debtor retained two or more financial advisors in cases with but a single committee.

If we limit our focus to the first committee appointed in the case – typically the basic unsecured creditors committee – in 51 cases that committee retained a single financial advisor, in four cases it retained two financial advisors.

Financial advisors – including turnaround consultants – are less likely to be retained by debtors in the smallest quartile of cases in the dataset. As shown on Table 25A, it also appears that multiple retentions are less likely to occur with respect to the smaller debtors.[183]

183 Cases with no financial advisors are omitted from the table to reduce the number of cells and increase the readability. Tables 25 and 25A will not match up exactly, since Table 25A includes cases without committees, unlike Table 25.

Table 25A: Combined Debtor and Committee Financial Advisor and Turnaround Consultant Retentions, by Debtor Size

	Number retained in case						
Debtor size by quartile	*1*	*2*	*3*	*4*	*5*	*6*	*Total*
(smallest) 1	8	3	1	0	0	0	12
2	7	7	4	1	1	1	21
3	3	7	9	3	0	0	22
4	4	4	10	1	2	0	21
Total	22	21	24	5	3	1	76

Cases with no retentions omitted

Table 26 shows the typical cost for financial advisors and turnaround consultants. For the 66 cases with at least one financial advisor or turnaround consultant, the extra cost associated with these averages $2.9 million, with a median cost of $1.6 million.[184] The debtor spends much more on these professionals than committees, with the average debtor spending $2.5 million as compared with $862,000 for committees. In other words, debtors spend an average of about three times as much on these professionals as committees do.[185]

Table 26: Cost of Financial Advisors and Turnaround Consultants

	Obs	*Mean*	*Std. Dev.*	*Median*	*Min*	*Max*
Debtor FA	51	$1,966,577.00	$2,296,789.00	$1,406,436.00	$3,232.26	$10,400,000.00
Debtor TC	23	$2,113,132.00	$3,232,314.00	$1,010,300.00	$152,947.90	$15,800,000.00
Debtor Total	59	$2,523,684.00	$3,767,882.00	$1,512,281.00	$3,875.04	$24,500,000.00
Committee FA	53	$862,493.20	$868,316.80	$554,448.00	$4,025.00	$3,028,514.00
All combined	66	$2,948,628.00	$4,206,185.00	$1,615,799.00	$3,875.04	$26,900,000.00

As shown in the top graph in Figure 27, in cases with both turnaround consultants and financial advisors, these professionals constitute the biggest portion of overall cost save for debtor's counsel, although the small number of such cases suggests the need for caution. And as also shown on the same graph, these professionals combined with bankruptcy counsel for the debtor and committee make up more than 71% of the overall cost of such a case. Turnaround consultants account for 17.27% of total cost, while financial advisors account for 17.05% of total cost.

184 The number of retained professionals in the following tables are often somewhat less than the total number of retentions discussed earlier, because in some cases the fee applications were missing from the docket. That is, in some cases I know a financial advisor or turnaround consultant was retained, but I do not know how much they were paid.

185 Debtors spend 2.6 times as much on a median basis.

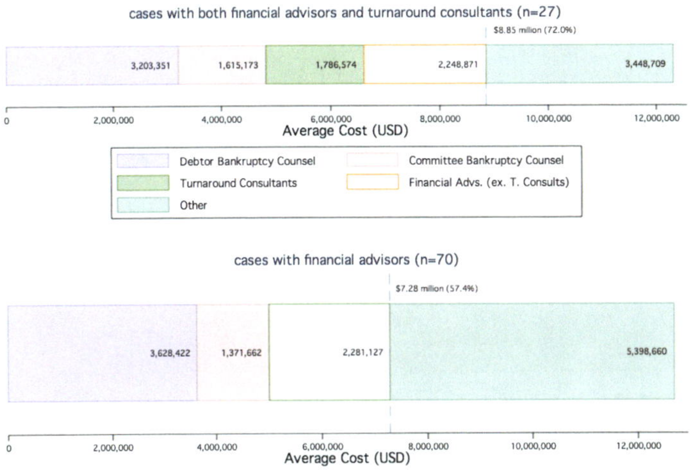

Figure 27: Components of Overall Chapter 11 Cost

The bottom graph in Figure 27 shows cases with financial advisors, whether or not there was a turnaround consultant. In this larger group, financial advisors account for 18.2% of average cost, and together with the attorneys these three groups of professionals represent almost 60% of the average total cost in the chapter 11 case. Financial advisors, although receiving much attention and criticism, actually cost slightly less, on average, than the debtor's bankruptcy attorneys.

The remaining 40% of professionals are comprised of a variety of lawyers, accountants, and other professionals. Some, like appraisers and real estate professionals, may be directly involved in the bankruptcy cases, while others may be exogenous to the bankruptcy process, like lawyers handling a specific piece of non-bankruptcy litigation or auditors that would have been retained even if there had never been a bankruptcy case. In the latter case, the professionals earn too much compensation to be retained under an OCP motion. Figure 28 shows the breakdown of these professionals. Attorneys retained under section 327(e) of the Code, that is, attorneys retained for a specific non-bankruptcy purpose, are the most common "other" professional.[186]

186 11 U.S.C. §327(e) ("The trustee, [and thus the debtor in possession] with the court's approval, may employ, for a specified special purpose, other than to represent the trustee in conducting the case, an attorney that has represented the debtor, if in the best interest of the estate, and if such attorney does not represent or hold any interest adverse to the debtor or to the estate with respect to the matter on which such attorney is to be employed."). This contrasts with the "normal" mode of retention, which is under section 327(a). 11 U.S.C. § 327(a) ("Except as otherwise provided in this section, the trustee, with the court's approval, may employ one or more attorneys, accountants, appraisers, auctioneers, or other professional persons, that do not hold

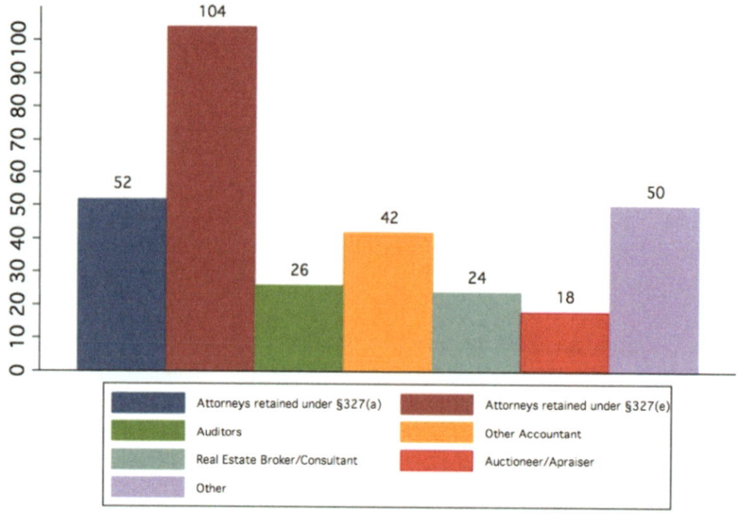

Figure 28: Frequencies of Other Professionals

B. Modeling the Cost of Financial Advisors

In the only other attempt to model financial advisors costs in chapter 11, LoPucki (2008) found that debtor size, filing in Delaware or New York, and the number of financial advisors retained in the case were the key factors ($p<0.05$) in predicting total financial advisor cost.[187] The authors also found that retention of KPMG LLP as a financial consultant reduced overall cost, although the implications of this finding are not discussed in the article.[188]

I begin by testing the LoPucki (2008) model on my data, using the same factors save for KPMG retention. In LoPucki (2008) all factors were positively related to total financial advisor cost, although time spent in chapter 11 was not significant. The authors report that Model II on Table 10 in LoPucki (2008) resulted in an adjusted R-squared of 0.68.

When applied to the present dataset, the LoPucki model achieves an adjusted R-squared (0.431). The two jurisdictional variables are not significant.

On Table 29 I develop my own model. In the first model I consider debtor size. This should be positively related to cost, but consistent with my prior stud-

or represent an interest adverse to the estate, and that are disinterested persons, to represent or assist the trustee in carrying out the trustee's duties under this title.")

187 The authors also found that their "trend" variable was significant ($p < 0.01$).

188 http://us.kpmg.com/services/content.asp?l1id=10&l2id=760.

ies of other aspects of chapter 11 costs, I would expect debtor size to decrease in import as the models begin to address complexity and other factors more directly.

In the second model I add a proxy for complexity, namely a dummy variable that indicates whether a claims agent was used in the case.[189] This should be positively correlated with cost.

In the third model, I add a dummy variable that indicates if both the debtor and the committees had at least one financial advisor. This reflects the insight from Table 29.1, which shows that there is often a kind of parallelism between debtor and committee retention of financial advisors. This variable thus indicates whether this is a case where this kind of joint retention is present.

Table 29.1: Number of Financial Advisors Retained

	Committees		
Debtor	*None*	*1 or more*	*Total*
None	26	15	41
1 or more	14	42	56
Total	40	57	97

In the final model I add the number of fee objections in the case to this model, log transformed and mean centered – that is, the mean is subtracted from every value.[190] I use this variable as an index of how contentious the case is, theorizing that these cases might be more likely to result in valuation disputes and other litigation and challenges to the financial advisors' work. The large lump sum fees that financial advisors and turnaround consultants receive might make them the likely targets of a case with more fee objections. And financial advisors typically pass on the cost of defending their retention and compensation in the bankruptcy court, which means that a more contentious case will result in another layer of attorneys' fees paid through the financial advisors' fee applications. By mean-centering the variable, the coefficient can now be interpreted as indicating the extra cost associated with above average "contentiousness." Cases with less than average contentiousness will have a negative value in this variable, which, combined with the positive coefficient shown on Table 29, results in lower overall financial advisor costs.

As in the other chapters, throughout this chapter I adjust the standard errors to account for potential, unseen correlations among cases within the same judicial district (*i.e.*, clustered standard errors).

189 Ordinary course professional motions are not used in this chapter, inasmuch as the financial advisors and turnaround consultants, unlike attorneys, would not be much affected by such a motion.

190 Log of a zero value is undefined. To account for the number of cases with zero objections, I also add a constant (0.001) to the total number of objections in all cases.

Table 29: Models of Total Financial Advisor Cost

	(1) Log of total TC & FA cost in case	(2) Log of total TC & FA cost in case	(3) Log of total TC & FA cost in case	(4) Log of total TC & FA cost in case
Log of debtor size	0.501*	0.317	0.234	0.236
	(0.185)	(0.173)	(0.136)	(0.124)
Claims agent		0.776**	0.566**	0.478**
		(0.258)	(0.197)	(0.173)
Both retained FA			0.844***	0.789***
			(0.197)	(0.172)
Log case objs, centered				0.142***
				(0.0381)
Constant	1.855	2.895*	3.181**	3.179**
	(1.521)	(1.321)	(1.004)	(0.930)
Observations	66	66	66	66
R2	0.246	0.390*	0.567***	0.644***

Robust standard errors in parentheses; se adjusted for clustering by district; mean VIF (model 4) 1.21
* $p < 0.05$, ** $p < 0.01$, *** $p < 0.001$

The final model explains 64.4% of the variance in total financial advisor and turnaround consultant costs, comparable to the models described in LoPucki (2008). The joint retention of financial advisors, case complexity, and the contentiousness of the case are all significant factors in the cost, after size and complexity are accounted for.

The first two models, which involve size and complexity, explain very little, which suggests most of the work is done by the variables added in the last two models.

C. The Debtors' Financial Advisors & Turnaround Consultants

As noted on Table 26, the bulk of the cost associated with financial advisors comes from the debtor's side of the case. Similarly, turnaround consultants are a debtor-only phenomenon. Accordingly, I use this section to explore an extension of the model developed on Table 29 to the specific issue of debtor financial advisors and turnaround consultants.

Table 30 shows that while turnaround consultants and financial advisors are often retained by the same debtor, the two are largely independent. In 12 cases there were turnaround consultants without financial advisors, and in 38 cases there were financial advisors without turnaround consultants, in 13 cases there were multiple financial advisors without any turnaround consultants. And in 29 cases the debtor retained neither.

Table 30: Number of Debtor Financial Advisors and Turnaround Consultants

	Financial Advisors				
Turnaround Consultants	0	1	2	3	*Total*
0	29	25	12	1	67
1	10	15	2	0	27
2	2	1	0	0	3
Total	41	41	14	1	97

I model debtor financial advisor cost (Model 1) and the combined cost of financial advisors and turnaround consultants (Model 2) on Table 31. In both cases I use a modified version of the final Model from Table 28, accounting for the change in dependent variables, which no longer includes committee financial advisors.

In particular, I enter measures of size, a proxy for complexity, and the measure of case contentiousness, the mean-centered number of fee objections in the case. I also use the dummy variable that indicates the retention of one or more turnaround consultants. In addition, in these models I use a variable that indicates if a committee was appointed in the case and another that counts the number of debtor financial advisors. I hypothesize that all variables should be positively related to cost in either model.

Table 31: Models of Debtor Fin. Advisor & Turnaround Consultant Cost

	(1) Log of Debtor FA cost	*(2)* Log of Debtor TC & FA cost
Log of debtor size	0.435**	0.363***
	(0.142)	(0.0737)
Claims agent	0.119	0.169
	(0.217)	(0.150)
Number of debtor FAs	-0.102	-0.0252
	(0.176)	(0.131)
Turnaround consultant	0.0654	0.327*
	(0.250)	(0.157)
Log of objs, mean centered	0.143***	0.134***
	(0.0353)	(0.0352)
Committee	0.834*	0.670*
	(0.327)	(0.281)
Constant	1.540	2.139**
	(0.925)	(0.599)
Observations	49	57
R2	0.691	0.681

Robust standard errors in parentheses; se adjusted for clustering by district; mean VIF 1.48 and 1.27, respectively.

* $p < 0.05$, ** $p < 0.01$, *** $p < 0.001$

The first model considers the cost of debtor financial advisors alone. Size, case contentiousness (number of fee objections), and an appointment of a committee are the key factors in this model. Interestingly, the number of debtor financial advisors is not significant, suggesting that it does not matter if the work is divided among multiple financial advisors. The appointment of a turnaround consultant also is not significant, suggesting that the cost of financial advisors is somewhat independent from the appointment of these related professionals.

The second model follows the LoPucki (2008) approach and considers the two types of debtor professionals in the aggregate, using the same model. The turnaround advisor variable is now significant, which is to be expected as the difference in the two dependent variables is the turnaround consultant cost.

Interestingly, in both models size is significant again. This may suggest a debtor-specific effect that was hidden when considering the joint cost of financial advisors in Table 29. For example, there may be an unmodeled element of complexity here – larger debtors may engage their financial advisors in different ways than smaller debtors.

Summary

This chapter examines the other big source of professional costs in chapter 11: financial advisors, and the subsidiary group of professionals known as "turnaround consultants." Almost 70% of the debtors, or 67 of 97 debtors, in the dataset retain at least one financial advisor or turnaround consultant, and an almost equal number retain more than one. Many committees also retained financial advisors.

For the 66 cases with at least one financial advisor or turnaround consultant, the extra cost associated with these averages $2.9 million, with a median cost of $1.6 million. The debtor spends much more on these professionals than committees, with the average debtor spending $2.5 million as compared with $862,000 for committees. In other words, debtors are spending an average of about three times as much as committees on these professionals. Perhaps most importantly, this chapter shows that the joint retention of financial advisors by the debtor and the committee results in increased cost

VII Summary and Conclusion

A. English Version

In this study I've examined both the very large chapter 11 cases that are the subject of much academic and popular attention, and the more typical chapter 11 cases that are numerically more common. In Chapters 3 and 4, the differences between these two types of chapter 11 cases were illuminated.

In particular, while very large chapter 11 cases operate on a very functional basis, often receiving court permission to deviate from the strict terms of the Bankruptcy Code with things like OCP motions, the average chapter 11 case deviates from conventional wisdom in the opposition direction. For example, many of these smaller chapter 11 cases do not even have creditors committees, and when they do have committees, the committee might not retain professionals. Additionally, the professionals in many of these case run the risk of non-payment, as conversion to chapter 7 or outright dismissal is a real possibility.

The models presented on Table 10 in Chapter 4 are the heart of the study. Through a combination of complexity and size, I show how more than 85% of a big chapter 11 case's direct costs can be explained. But this section also highlights the difficult questions that lurk in any examination of chapter 11 debtors. For example, what exactly do we consider when we examine a debtor's "size," and what aspect of size is really complexity that is independent of, although heavily associated with, size?

In Chapters 5 and 6, I expand the study beyond the traditional focus on cost in the aggregate, to consider two of the biggest individual elements of chapter 11 costs. Chapter 5 looks at the cost of bankruptcy counsel, both comprehensively and as incurred by debtors and committees separately. Chapter 5 shows that bankruptcy attorneys, at least from the biggest cities in the United States, operate in a nationwide market, often handling cases across the country from their home jurisdiction. This chapter also shows that committee counsel has a positive effect on how much a debtor spends on its own bankruptcy counsel.

In Chapter 6 I turn to financial advisors and turnaround consultants. I also provide some basic information on the myriad "other" professionals retained in a chapter 11 case. Here I show that parallel retention of financial advisors by both the committee and the debtor increase overall cost. The size of the debtor positively increases the debtor's own financial advisor costs, suggesting that larger debtors use financial advisors in a different way than other debtors.

* * *

In the United States, chapter 11 continues to attract a good deal of attention, as large debtors like Lehman Brothers, General Motors, and Washington Mutual pay millions of dollars – in Lehman, perhaps as much as $1 billion – to work their way through bankruptcy. The sheer numbers involved, stacked against the losses suffered, often lead to heated claims that professionals do little in chapter 11 but loot the estate.[191]

But these impressionist endeavors provide little actual understanding of how much chapter 11 costs. And how much chapter 11 costs is important both internationally and domestically as policymakers increasingly struggle to develop tools that will mitigate the effects of financial distress.

In this study I have presented three broad categories of models: models of the total cost of chapter 11, models of attorney costs, and models of financial advisor costs. With these new tools it becomes possible to examine past and future chapter 11 costs, and compare those costs with other possible solutions.

Along the way I find that

- Time spent in chapter 11 has no relationship with cost once a fully specified model is considered.
- References to a professional's "burn rate" are thus misleading, inasmuch as it implies a fixed or constant cost to chapter 11. Costs ebb and flow through the course of the case.
- Prepackaged chapter 11 cases are not significantly cheaper than regular chapter 11 cases.
- Cases filed in New York or Delaware do not cost more – in fact, these jurisdictions seem to actually reduce chapter 11 costs, likely because of their greater experience with complex chapter 11 cases.
- Fee examiners do not reduce the costs of big chapter 11 cases.
- Complexity and the compensation structure of the professionals retained, which may itself reflect further aspects of complexity, are the key determinants of cost. Debtor size is but a loose proxy for these factors, but is itself of reduced relevance once a fuller model is developed.
- Complexity is associated with economies of scale, resulting in lower chapter 11 costs for the very largest, most complex cases.

I thus conclude with the hope that this study will be but the beginning of a more subtle, less combative examination of chapter 11. Given the current economic reality, the debate is of special import.

B. Dutch Version/Nederlandse versie

In dit onderzoek heb ik zowel de zeer grote ondernemingen die een reorganisatie onder regie van chapter 11 van de Amerikaanse Faillissementswet (Bankruptcy Code) uitvoeren – en welke onderwerp zijn van veel wetenschappelijke en popu-

191 Lynn M. LoPucki & Joseph W. Doherty, *Professional Overcharging in Large Bankruptcy Reorganization Cases*, 5 J. Empirical L.. Stud. 983 (2008).

laire aandacht – en de meer typische kleinere ondernemingen in chapter 11, die getalsmatig vaker voorkomen, onderzocht. In de hoofdstukken 3 en 4 worden de belangrijkste verschillen tussen deze twee soorten van ondernemingen in chapter 11 belicht.

In het bijzonder valt op dat de zeer grote ondernemingen in chapter 11 opereren op een zeer functionele basis en vaak van de rechter toestemming ontvangen om af te wijken van de strikte voorwaarden van de Bankruptcy Code onder andere met zogenaamde "OCP motions". De gemiddelde onderneming in chapter 11 wijkt af van de conventionele wijsheid in juist de andere richting. Veel van de kleinere ondernemingen hebben niet eens een commissie van schuldeisers. Wanneer ze een dergelijke commissie hebben dan heeft deze veelal niet de beschikking over professionele adviseurs. Daarnaast lopen adviseurs in deze zaken het risico van non-betaling, omdat een overheveling naar chapter 7 of zelfs ontslag een reële mogelijkheid is.

De modellen gepresenteerd in tabel 10 in hoofdstuk 4 vormen het hart van de studie. Door een combinatie van complexiteit en omvang, laat ik zien dat meer dan 85% van de directe kosten van grote ondernemingen in chapter 11 kan worden verklaard. Maar er wordt ook gewezen op de moeilijke vragen die schuilen in elk onderzoek naar grote ondernemingen in chapter 11. Bijvoorbeeld wat wordt precies beschouwd wanneer omvang wordt onderzocht, en welk aspect van omvang is eigenlijk te bezien als complexiteit dat onafhankelijk is, maar toch in grote mate gerelateerd aan, omvang?

In de hoofdstukken 5 en 6 heb ik de studie uitgebreid buiten de traditionele focus op de totale kosten van chapter 11, en wel naar twee van de grootste afzonderlijke kostenposten van chapter 11. Hoofdstuk 5 beziet de kosten van een "bankruptcy counsel" (faillissementsadvocaten), zowel in haar geheel als ook afzonderlijk voor debiteuren en commissies. Hoofdstuk 5 laat zien dat de kantoren van faillissement-advocaten, althans in de grootste steden in de Verenigde Staten, opereren op een nationale markt, en vaak ook zaken behandelen in het hele land vanuit de eigen thuis jurisdictie. Dit hoofdstuk laat ook zien dat de advocaten van een schuldeiserscommissie een positief effect hebben op hoeveel een schuldenaar zelf uitgeeft aan haar eigen advocaten.

In hoofdstuk 6 staan de financiële adviseurs en "turnaround consultants" centraal. Ook is er enige informatie over de talloze "andere" professionals die worden ingeschakeld bij een onderneming in chapter 11. Hier laat ik zien dat de parallelle inschakeling van financiële adviseurs door zowel een schuldeiserscommissie als de schuldenaar tot een verhoging van de totale kosten leidt. De omvang van de schuldenaar heeft een positief effect op de kosten van de eigen financieel adviseurs. Dit suggereert dat grote ondernemingen financiële adviseurs op een andere manier gebruiken dan andere schuldenaren.

* * *

In de Verenigde Staten blijft de regeling van chapter 11 veel aandacht trekken, vooral ook omdat grote ondernemingen als Lehman Brothers, General Motors, en

Washington Mutual vele miljoenen dollars betalen – in Lehman, misschien wel 1 miljard dollar – om hun weg te vinden door de procedure. Deze enorme bedragen, met daarbij de geleden verliezen voor betrokkenen, leiden vaak tot verhitte discussies waarin gesteld wordt dat de professionals weinig doen in chapter 11, behalve de boedel leegroven.

Maar deze impressionistische verhalen bieden weinig inzicht in de werkelijke omvang van de kosten van chapter 11. En deze kosten zijn van belang omdat zowel internationaal als in eigen land beleidsmakers in toenemende mate worden uitgedaagd om hulpmiddelen te ontwikkelen die de gevolgen van financiële nood verminderen.

In deze studie heb ik drie brede categorieën van modellen gepresenteerd: modellen van de totale kosten van chapter 11, modellen van de kosten van advocaten, en modellen van de kosten van financieel adviseurs. Met deze modellen is het mogelijk om zowel historische als toekomstige chapter 11 kosten te onderzoeken, en te vergelijken met de kosten van andere mogelijke oplossingen.

De belangrijkste bevindingen zijn:

- Zodra een volledig gespecificeerd model wordt gehanteerd, heeft de tijd die een onderneming doorbrengt in chapter 11 geen relatie meer met de kosten.
- Verwijzingen naar een zogenaamde "burn rate" van professionals is dus misleidend, daar het vaste of constante kosten voor chapter 11 veronderstelt. Kosten nemen echter toe en af in relatie tot het beloop van de zaak.
- "Prepackaged" chapter 11 gevallen zijn niet significant goedkoper dan de reguliere chapter 11 gevallen.
- Zaken aanhangig gemaakt in de staten New York of Delaware kosten niet meer dan elders – in feite lijken deze rechtsgebieden de kosten te verminderen, waarschijnlijk vanwege hun grotere ervaring met complexe chapter 11 gevallen.
- "Fee examiners" verminderen niet de kosten van grote chapter 11 gevallen.
- Complexiteit en beloningsstructuur van de advocaten, welke mogelijk ook aspecten van complexiteit van de onderneming zijn, zijn de belangrijkste determinanten van de kosten. Omvang van de debiteur is een soort van substituut voor deze factoren, en neemt dan ook in belang af indien deze factoren in een meer omvangrijk model worden gespecificeerd.
- Complexiteit kent ook schaalvoordelen; lagere kosten resulteren voor de allergrootste, meest complexe gevallen.

Ik sluit met de hoop uit te spreken dat deze studie het begin zal zijn van een meer subtiele, minder strijdlustige analyse van chapter 11. Gezien de huidige economische realiteit is een dergelijk debat meer dan ooit noodzakelijk.